An Unbreakable Bond

Finding God's Grace Through Our Brokenness

Richard Williams

Carl E. Roberts

An Unbreakable Bond
ISBN: Softcover 979-8-89532-018-1
Copyright © 2024 by Richard Williams

All Scripture quotations are from either the New Living Translation (1996) by Tyndale House Foundation or the English Standard Version (2001) by Crossway unless otherwise noted.

Parson's Porch Books is an imprint of Parson's Porch *&* Company (PP*&*C) in Cleveland, Tennessee. PP*&*C is a self-funded charity which earns money by publishing books of noted authors, representing all genres. Its face and voice is **David Russell Tullock** (dtullock@parsonsporch.com).

Parson's Porch *&* Company *turns books into bread & milk* by sharing its profits with the poor.

www.parsonsporch.com

An Unbreakable Bond

Dedication

I grew up in an era when real men did not attend church. Sundays were reserved for football games, or hunting and fishing and it was left to the women to take the children to church. In 1996 I had invited Reggie White of the Philadelphia Eagles to speak at our chapel service for the homeless and addicted people from off the streets of Chester, Pennsylvania. Two gentlemen sitting on the front row of the chapel made the mistake of trying to heckle this giant of a man. Reggie looked them both square in the eyes and made the following comment, "You think you are real men, don't you? Well, I am here to tell you that you are not. It takes a real man to follow Jesus; a real man who can stand up against those who blindly make fun of Jesus; a real man who will go against the tide of a society that shows disdain for anyone who would dare call Jesus Lord."

This book is dedicated to three such men who, like Reggie White, have played a significant role in me becoming the man I am today.

To Dr. Jack Snodgrass and Logan Cothern who taught a young sixteen-year-old boy filled with anger and rage what the true meaning of grace meant. They used no words but walked it out in front of that confused boy standing in front of a judge facing the possibility of ten years in prison. They forever changed the course of direction of this young man by believing in him when he could not believe in himself.

To Carl E Roberts who for many years has poured into my spiritual life. Much of what has been written in the book has been influenced by the spiritual truths these men have taught me. I am truly blessed to call them my brothers.

Contents

Foreword

In the summer of 1972 after graduating high school, I started working a job that would allow me to work the summer and then adjust my schedule to work around my college classes in the fall. This is where I first met Richard Williams. As we worked together, we almost immediately became friends. There was just something about him that was different. I didn't know what it was at the time, but it later became very clear to me as I watched his interaction with others in various circumstances of life. Richard is someone who has the ability to put people at ease and make them feel comfortable around him. It doesn't matter if it's the bank president or some strange motorist on the side of the road, they both get the same treatment from Richard.

Someone once said, "People won't care how much you know, until they know how much you care." Richard has a genuine concern for the well-being of others and a compassion for their needs. When Richard sees someone in need, whether it's a physical, financial, or spiritual need, He goes into what I call "Richard Mode" where he is working the problem and seeking help and offering assistance to meet that particular need.

Richard very generously credits me with helping to lead him to the Lord. However, the man that I knew and grew to love as a brother, was hungry for the love of God and the peace that He brings. I don't believe anyone, or anything could have stopped him from accepting Christ as the Master of his life. I have watched him in his witness for Christ over the last fifty years.

He continues to place hungry needy people in the light of God's love, so that they might share in the grace of God.

Through his own personal struggles, a pattern began to emerge:

> You ask for the forgiveness of your sins and invite Christ into your life.
> You start down this new path with good intentions.
> Then life gets in the way.
> You find yourself doing the old things, acting the old ways, saying the old things. You struggle,
> You repent,
> You repeat and start the cycle over again.

This book deals with this struggle that all Christians face. As you read it, I believe you will be enlightened, challenged, and surprised. You may not agree with some of these concepts. It may challenge some of your paradigms. It may give you a different point of view. Every concept in this book is backed up by Scripture.

If you are seeking a continuous unbroken relationship with God, this book guides you through a step-by-step process beginning with Chapter One. This chapter shows that it starts with being *broken* and surrendering *everything* to God. Each of the following chapters builds on the former, until you find yourself in the center of God's Will. Isn't that where we want to be? The problem with too many Christians is that we want to be on the fringe of Christianity and enjoy the blessings of

God's love yet stay on the edge and continue to dabble in the ways of the world.

But wait, if you were in a shooting contest, you wouldn't aim for the edge of the target. You would aim for the bullseye. We should be aiming for the center of God's will.

After reading this book and studying the scriptures you will have gained the ability and have the tools to claim your right to an unbroken relationship with God. Then the question becomes not, Can I have an unbroken relationship with God? Instead, it becomes, *Will I?*

Mike Boling, a friend

Endorsements

In the Introduction to his latest book, *An Unbreakable Bond: Finding God's Grace through our Brokenness*, my friend and colleague Richard Williams, asks an extremely penetrating spiritual question which we should all be asking ourselves: "Is it, or is it not possible to have total and complete victory in every aspect of our lives, starting today?" If you are not sure of the answer to that question, I strongly recommend this powerful book for you. In chapter after chapter, Richard makes the point that it's not just about total salvation in the by-and-by when we all get to heaven. It's about total joyous victorious living day by day in the here and now, despite those life experiences that are designed by the Evil One to break our relationship with God and cause us to sin again and again. Richard's challenge to this victorious living is for those for whom the struggle to *"be holy as I am holy,"* has been one of striving, stumbling, repenting, and repeating the process. He freely admits that much of his life has been about just that - striving, stumbling, repenting, and repeating the process. "But it doesn't have to be that way," he boldly declares. Studying Scripture after Scripture, he shows us that God's plan and the price He paid for our salvation are so that we can live a life of total and complete victory, starting today.

Because of having known Richard well for almost forty years, I can tell you that he is a man with a profound passion to know God in a deep and personal way and to live for Christ in complete victory and holiness. In *An Unbreakable Bond,* he lays bare his soul - his struggles, his failures, and his relentless quest for victory. Richard is no armchair theologian. His theology has been forged by the many struggles and hardships through which he has held tightly to God's promise of victory for each and every day. I have watched again and again, as yet another seemingly insurmountable trial has pounded him. But it has been through the crucible of those devastating challenges that the man Richard is today was formed. A man after God's own heart.

In this book, Richard opens those Scriptures, many of which we have often glossed over, that speak to the reality of a life lived in victory and holiness. The answer to that all-important question with which he begins this book is a resounding "Yes! It is possible to have total and complete victory in every aspect of our lives, starting today. He shares how it is only through our brokenness before God, when we fall in total repentance and complete surrender before Jesus, that a life of holiness and daily victory over sin is possible. So, don't fall into the trap of thinking, as we frequently do, "Well, I'm only human," or "I can make it if I only try harder." Journey with Richard through *An Unbreakable Bond,* as he walks you through the Scriptures that will lead you to a life of incredible victory that you never thought possible on this side of heaven.

David F. Hunt, DMin
Disciple Making Movements
Mentor and Coach

An Unbreakable Bond is nothing short of life-changing! In a world where distractions and doubt pull at the very fabric of our faith, Richard masterfully illuminates the path to a deep, unshakeable relationship with God. Grounded entirely in Scripture, this book offers more than just theory. It is a guide to transforming your walk with God. Richard doesn't just tell you what is possible, he shows you how to achieve An Unbreakable Bond with the Father through the wisdom of God's Word.

For every Christian who longs for a closer more intimate relationship with God, *An Unbreakable Bond* is the answer. Whether you have felt distant or just desire more of Him, this book will reignite your passion for God's presence and fill you with confidence that an unbreakable relationship with God is not just a dream – it is His promise. It is rare to find a work that speaks so directly to the heart and soul of modern believers, yet in *An Unbreakable Bond,* Richard does just that.

I can personally say that this book has deepened my connection with God in ways I didn't think were possible. It is a must read for anyone seeking to live in the fullness of God's love and presence. If you are ready to step into a new level of faith and intimacy with the Father, *An Unbreakable Bond* will show you the way.

Brandon Maxey
A disciple in progress

Richard has put together a message that humility and brokenness are the way to receive grace and intimacy with God. If you are on a quest for unbroken intimacy, connection, and communion with God, this book will help you on your journey.

Marty Mattocks
Retired Information Technology Manager
Disciple-Making Movement Practitioner and Trainer

I confess that I do not know the Scriptures the way that Richard knows them and uses them.

How refreshing it is to read his words about knowing God and the need to work on an unbroken relationship with our Creator. Richard's knowledge of the Scriptures is very meaningful to a neophyte like me. It produces the desired reaction to want to know more. He makes it clear that it is a lifelong journey, and we must make space in our busy lives for seeking God. We all need much more intimate relationship with our Creator. Richard makes it abundantly clear that we must give ourselves to God, and that He will cause us to become spiritually hungry and thirsty for more of Him. You need to read this book!

William B. Strine, President
Media Real Estate

One of the most noteworthy radio commentators of the middle of the past century was Paul Harvey: charming, eloquent, and well informed. He had a daily feature at the start of which he winsomely told a true story about an event or person. Often the story was well-known. After completing the story there would be a break and then he would relate lesser-known ramifications about the event which were always interesting and unexpected, and added substantial meaning and relevance to the story. This feature was called *The Rest of the Story*.

An Unbreakable Bond is in that mold. The story of the redeeming act of Christ in death and resurrection is well known but often told in part. To be certain, embracing the suffering of Jesus on our behalf assures us of forgiveness of sin and restoration of relationship with God, especially as it pertains to certainty of our place with Him in heaven forever. But that is only part of God's purpose and gift. Less well known and celebrated is God's welcome into a heaven-like and stable relationship here and now which transforms believers into a life of discipleship and victorious living. Rich, in *An Unbreakable Bond* tells the rest of the story.

Joel Krott, Bachelor of Music
Director of Music, First Presbyterian Church, Moorestown, N.J.
Artistic Director, West Jersey Chamber of Music Society

In *An Unbreakable Bond* Richard Williams profoundly explores how our brokenness can lead us into a deeper relationship with God. Drawing from personal experiences and Biblical wisdom, this heartfelt work challenges readers to examine their own lives and relationship with God. *An Unbreakable Bond* encourages the reader to reimagine a life connected to God the

Father and assures that it is precisely in our struggles that we can encounter the profound grace and love of our Creator. It is a must-read for anyone wavering in faith or those seeking to deepen their relationship with God through the lens of their own broken spirit.

Dr. Kasey L. Trill
Assistant Professor of Nursing, West Chester University

In a world where the strength of our faith is often tested by the turmoil of our circumstances, Richard offers a beacon of hope and profound insight. This compelling book delves deeply into the core of Christian resilience and the unbreakable bond between believers and their Creator. Drawing upon rich insights and lived experiences, Richard illuminates the path to a steadfast and unshakeable relationship with God.

At the core of this book lies a transformative message: our external circumstances should never dictate the state of our faith, or our relationship with God. Richard powerfully explores this concept, reminding us that, like Paul, we are called to embrace an unbroken relationship with God, regardless of the trials and adversities that we face. Richard's writing resonates deeply with the reader as we learn that this divine equipping is not merely theoretical but intensely practical, offering a blueprint for living out a faith that transcends the issues of life.

For anyone grappling with the complexities of their faith or seeking a deeper, more intimate connection with God,

Richard's book is an essential read. It offers clarity, encouragement, and a renewed perspective on the profound truth that our relationship with God is not only unbreakable but also deeply fulfilling. In a time when many feel disheartened by life's challenges, this book is a testament to the victory we can experience through Christ's unwavering love and power.

Bill Coble, Founder,
Start with One International, Inc.

Richard and I have known each other for a short period of time, but our friendship runs very deep. Richard's writings have inspired me to study Gods Word even deeper. To know Richard has been a true blessing to me. His compassion for God and his salvation is very evident in this book and the way he lives his life. I highly recommend this book to anyone that wants to have a better understanding of how you can have a closer relationship with God.

Charles Snelson,
CMSGT, US Air Force, Retired

In Richard's book, *An Unbreakable Bond,* he challenges you to push past the barriers, tune out the noise, and in that sacred space of seeking, you will find your Lord and Savior. To seek a one-on-one relationship with the King of the universe. Richard explains how Christ came for much more than the forgiveness of sin. The ultimate purpose was to restore an intimate relationship with God the Father. Throughout this book, Richard guides you on how to walk out that relationship with God, to truly know Him, not to just know about Him. As you read and dive into what God has laid on Richard's heart, I encourage you to come with a heart to KNOW THE FATHER on a personal level and to surrender all.

Rachel Kent
Compassion for Life
Prayer Coordinator

I think some people can agree that many western Christians are nominal believers at best, speaking of Jesus with their lips but their lives revealing only barren branches devoid of good fruit. Those *some people* mentioned above may realize that they themselves are among the many who are going through the motions of being a follower of Jesus with little or no Kingdom impact. This, in direct contrast to those disciples who follow Jesus with wild abandoned love for Him and others in daily surrendered lives in nations hostile to the Gospel. If the former description is indicative of your life right now (although there may be some fear to truly admit it), then you are invited to *throw off the dead grave clothes* with each chapter of Richard's new book *An Unbreakable Bond,* and enter into true intimacy with God, full of the expectation that you, yes YOU, an ordinary person, can do great things with God, (not works-driven for God) in a joyous, living and vibrant, one-on-one personal relationship with God who loves you. Selah!

Elaine Mattocks
Missionary and Disciple-Making Practioner

Introduction

For the past twenty plus years I have traveled throughout the world training pastors and church leaders how to equip the church, (those sheep He has been called to shepherd) for the purpose of ministry. It was during this time that the Pew Foundation began doing an annual report on the state of Christian Religion in America. That report has shown that what in the beginning was a gradual decline in both church attendance and influence in our country, has now escalated into a collision course, with the church in America rapidly moving toward irrelevance. With the average age of today's church goer being in the late sixties to early seventies, coupled with a dramatic decline of all other ages, the traditional church is rapidly disappearing in America. This collision course became such a concern to the Pew Foundation that several years ago they made the bold statement that "within the next few years the Christian church in North America would become irrelevant." Their bold statement is proving to be prophetic.

At the same time, while trying to sound the alarm about this in my seminars, I am often asked why we do not see the fullness of God's power manifested in America. For example, if Jesus commanded us in Luke 10 to heal the sick, then why are the sick not being healed? Why is it that we do not see the power of the Holy Spirit working in the church today? Deep within me, I wondered why, in the face of adversity, people's faith could not sustain them? I was always prepared with a good theological response, but in my heart, it even left me feeling inadequate. I knew that the answer was much more serious than just a lack of faith. I also knew that the consequences were extremely grave.

This began to bother me so much that I asked two brothers that I have leaned into for years for Biblical wisdom to join me in searching God's Words for the answers. What is God's desire for the church? More importantly, what is God's desire for us? Not just when we get to heaven, but now. Is it, or is it not possible to have total and complete victory in every aspect of our lives, starting today?

It never fails that when I am doing a seminar, I can always count on being confronted with the question "why are we not seeing the manifestation of the Holy Spirit moving in the Church today?" More importantly, why is the church declining in America? Any accountant understands that if you get one number wrong in any equation, you are going to fall short of having a true result. These are questions that demand we get the spiritual equation correct.

"Several years ago, Andrew Murray wrote a book titled, *Abide in Him*. The premise of the book was abiding in Christ in a very intimate and powerful way. But is it really possible to have a relationship with God that is defined by the word intimate? Is it really possible to possess some sort of spiritual power as a result of that intimate relationship. With all my heart I have always desired that intimate, real relationship. But when I looked at my life it seemed no matter how hard I tried, I continued to live a life of striving, stumbling, repenting, and repeating the process. That process caused me not only to fail God, but at times fail the people I loved, as well as many others who looked to me as a spiritual leader. I asked myself over and over, "where is the victorious life that is presented in the Bible?" As a leader of an international ministry, I have the opportunity to meet many different people from all walks of life. Among them are many pastors and missionaries. When given the opportunity I would ask them about their personal walk with God. It always seemed that after further talks, their lives were not any different from mine. Is it possible that you, the reader, may be in the same boat?

In time I began to accept that the Christian life is just one of striving, stumbling, repenting, and repeating; that we really are just poor sinners saved by grace and as long as we live in these mortal bodies there will not be complete victory. But in my spirit, I just could not accept this.

Down deep, when I came to Christ, I felt like I had visited the Promised Land. I saw the milk and honey and wanted to take possession of it like I was supposed to. However, when I would ask others how to possess it, I only ran into people like the ten spies who were confident that it could not be done. I could not find any Joshua's or Caleb's. So, it seemed I was destined to wander the rest of my Christian life in the dessert. Nevertheless, I could not reconcile the many Scriptures that talked about the victory we could walk in now, in this life here on earth. As a result, I began spending more and more time asking God, "what am I missing? Why can I not obtain this victory that the Bible talks about?" Up to this point, all the ways I had approached the Christian life seemed right, but they were not producing real vibrant life in my relationship with God, and I knew it.

This book is about how God brought together people in my life from different backgrounds, trainings, and religious upbringing with over fifteen combined decades of seeking God. He is showing me the path to real victorious living, as well as how to stay on that path. This book comes from a viewpoint that we can't give to others what we do not possess ourselves. It is not about theological theory, or a debate about spiritual ideas. It is about how to have a real unbroken relationship with God the Father.

There is a story in Greek mythology about the Sirens of the Sea. The sirens were half beautiful women and half fish. When ships would pass through that area of the sea the sailors would jump overboard and try to swim to these beautiful creatures. Instead, they swam to their death. One captain's approach to combating this was to have his men tie him to the mast of the ship. No matter how much he might scream and demand to be cut loose, they were to leave him tied to the mast until they had safely sailed passed through that area of the sea where the sirens lived.

Another captain's approach was to have all his men begin to sing as they approached the sirens. The men would become so involved in singing that they never heard the sirens calling. The story ends by stating that the sirens were never heard from again.

My approach to the Christian life was like that of the captain who was tied to the mast. What do I mean by that? Being tied to the mast of the ship means never finding a resolution to the problem. Consequently, it meant that each time he sailed into that area the captain would have to endure the same struggle. His only hope would be that somehow when he faced that situation again it would become easier. He may choose to avoid sailing through that area as much as possible, but each time he passed through the struggle was the same. Seeing no other solution, he must accept his fate and continue to repeat the process. This cycle would ultimately lead to discouragement, doubt, and even despair.

But what would happen if he were shown a different approach? An approach that would solve the problem once and for all? That is what the other captain discovered. His approach was to find something else that the men would get so involved with and captivated by, that there would be no pull or temptation by the sirens.

How are we tied to the mast in the Christian walk? It is by taking paths that seem right but do not lead to the right destiny. For me it was taking the path that the way to please God was to be the very best that I could be with the help of the Holy Spirit. I tried by asking the Holy Spirit to make my old nature better. That was never God's plan.

The Father's plan was to send Jesus so we could be reconciled to Him and begin an unbroken relationship as He intended when He created mankind; a relationship that freed us from our old nature and a new spiritual nature becomes available to us. Once we are reconciled to that new nature, we can commune with God spirit to Spirit instead of flesh to Spirit.

When I realized what was most important to God and made that the most important thing to me, my life was eternally changed. I began walking down this new path in a new nature. As a result, God changed me from the inside out. I was no longer trying to do the impossible, which was to make my old nature better. I began to live in my new nature which was made available to me through Christ when He paid the price to reconcile me with God. I now live in a direct relationship with the Creator of the universe.

To put this in perspective, the purpose of the Bible, as well as Christ's coming to earth can be explained in the final words spoken by the Father just before people were eternally separated from God. "I never knew you, depart from me." (Matthew 7:23 KJV). God created us to be personally known by Him.

When we begin to experience an unbroken relationship with God – everything changes. We start down the right path. This book documents how this happened in my life. It is your invitation to taste and see for yourself. Once you have tasted for yourself – you will know.

Carl E Roberts and I met when he began attending a Sunday School class I taught almost forty years ago. Within a few short weeks I realized the wrong person was teaching the class. He was a walking Strong's Concordance. I could ask him to quote almost any verse in the Bible and without hesitation, he could recall it from memory, just like he had just been waiting for you to ask. Not only could he quote it, but he could also tell you the Greek or Hebrew translation of it and how it was to apply to the believer's life. Here is what this ardent student of God's Word would have you take away from this book.

"For much of my Christian life I thought it was about *doing*. I was *doing* all the things I thought believers were supposed to be doing. I wrongly perceived Christianity as accomplishing certain task; I thought we were supposed to

- Pray
- Tithe
- Attend church
- Read AND study the Bible
- Witness

The list goes on, and I must admit I thought I was *doing* a decent job. However, by the grace of God over these past two years I have come to the truth of Scripture. That truth, in simple terms is that God did not save me just so that I could go to Heaven! He saved me so that He could have a relationship with me. Sin in our lives blunts that relationship. Jesus' act on Calvary took care of those sins. The purpose of forgiving our sins was not so that I could go to heaven, but rather that I could have a relationship with God the Father. Heaven is a fringe benefit. It should be noted here that we are not saved by praying a certain prayer or signing a church commitment card, or even kneeling at an altar. We are taught in Ephesians 2:8 and 9 that we are saved by trusting in what Jesus did on Calvary. We understand that believing this will bring a certain corresponding action in our life. That action is called repentance. When I came to this realization of scriptural truth, I was changed from focusing on *doing* and transitioned into *being* in direct relationship with my Heavenly Father. I no longer *do things* because that is what a Christian is supposed to do. I would describe my life now as a f*low*. The things I do now is relationship driven instead of required. This is a massive difference. The change is that now I am living in a world where the Holy Spirit has so consumed me, God consciousness is dominant within me at all times. His presence is so real, I simply *flow* in this world. Christianity is not a world of *doing* to please God. Instead, it is a world where we *flow* as one with the Holy Spirit."

Carl and others have greatly influenced the writing of this book as we have journeyed together on a quest for Biblical truth. Early on I realized we were not put together for the sake of discovering Biblical healing, or the use of any of the other spiritual gifts listed in the Bible. It would not be about more theological Biblical knowledge. Our quest would be to understand the heart of the One who had all the authority of both heaven and earth. If we answered that question, everything else pertaining to Scripture would be answered as well.

For over two years we have met together seeking to wholeheartedly know God in ways we had never known Him before, even after each of us knowing Him for almost fifty years. We are simply men that have faithfully followed the Lord all those years. Yet inwardly we wondered why we did not see more of the power, more of the victory that was spoken of in Scripture over and over. We are still on the journey, but each day is bringing us closer to possessing the real Pearl of great price. It is my desire to invite you on this journey with us as we seek to find the fullness of God. It is the *Pearl of Great Price, the Treasure hidden beneath the soil.* (Matthew chapter 13).

Chapter One
Hunger and Thirst for God

Jesus replied, I am the bread of life. Whoever comes to me will never be hungry again. Whoever believes in me will never be thirsty. John 6:35

A friend had lamented to me, "I had hungered and thirsted for most of my life, but something was missing. The Bible talks about spiritual victory, why could I not obtain and sustain it?" How do we enter into a real unbroken relationship with God? How do we transition from striving, stumbling, repenting, and repeating?

If you desire more in your relationship with God, if you want a continuous unbroken relationship with the Creator, here is where it must begin: no more striving in the flesh, no more stumbling and falling, no more repenting only to repeat the process over and over again. If you feel there is more of God that you need, if you sense there is more of you that God wants, let's explore how to get there.

Research and study have shown that the human body can go for about three weeks without nourishment. After that it begins to shut down and we eventually die. The same is true of water with the exception that death occurs much more rapidly. The body begins to shut down after only three days. The same is true of our spiritual relationship with God. If we are not drinking from the *well that never runs dry*, if we are not feasting on God's Word and seeking Him through earnest prayer, then at best we become spiritually anemic, at worst we spiritually die. As we die physically without proper nutrition, so we risk spiritual death without proper spiritual nourishment.

Hunger and thirst are natural responses built into our bodies to make sure we properly care for them. The same is true of us spiritually. If we have truly given ourselves to God, He causes us to become spiritually hungry and thirsty for more of Him. It is not a case where I must force myself to spiritually eat and drink, but rather a natural result of the Holy Spirit living within me. This is designed to keep us from becoming spiritually anemic or even risking that spiritual death because of spiritual starvation. This is the meaning behind Matthew 5:6 (NIV), *"Blessed are those who hunger and thirst for righteousness for they shall be filled."* In that same chapter in verse 13 Jesus said, *"You are the salt of the earth, but if the salt loses its saltiness, how can it be made salty again? It is no longer good for anything, but to be thrown out and trampled underfoot."* If we are not feasting at the feet of Jesus, we become powerless and useless to God.

I want us to take a look at one man in the Bible who I believe illustrates what it means to hunger and thirst for God. There are several men in the Old Testament who loomed large in the eyes of God. Men like Abraham to whom God made a vow to make him the father of many nations; Joseph who went from a pit to being one God used to keep his people from starving to death. There was Noah who was found to be the only righteous man on earth, and Moses who led Israel from bondage to the Promise Land. But there was only one man that

God ever said, *"this is a man after my own heart."* That man was David, who started life as a lowly sheepherder. What was it about David that would draw such a statement from God? It certainly wasn't his perfect record of never disappointing God. It wasn't because he had lived a sinless life. The truth is that David had committed some of the most egregious sins that a human being could ever commit. David struggled with the sin of lust which led him to commit adultery with another man's wife. A lot of so-called Christians would have turned their backs on David right then and shunned him. Then if that wasn't bad enough David actually took the time to devise a plot to cover up his sin by having the husband of the woman killed. Here we have a picture of a man who was guilty of deceit, lust, adultery, and murder. How is it that such a person could become a man after God's own heart?

The answer to this question can be found at least in part in Psalm 51. I am almost compelled to write out this entire Psalm as I think that David's cry to God here shows the ultimate brokenness he came to in his walk with God. For the sake of time, I will extract some key verses to write about, but please, if you truly want an unbroken relationship with God read the entire Psalm multiple times and ask God to reveal to you the secret that led David to that unbroken relationship with his Lord. I will tell you now what that secret was. It was his brokenness over what he had done. However, I want you to see it from David's words in what he wrote here, and not because of my writing about it. Look for David's heart.

In the first seven verses David is confessing his sins. You can very clearly tell that his heart is heavy, not because he fears God's wrath, which he admits he deserves, but because he has caused a separation between himself and God. That separation causes a hunger within him to be restored, and it was that hunger that led him to cry out these words in verse eight, "*oh give me back my joy again; you have broken me.*" (emphasis mine). The equation here is this: brokenness of heart equals unbrokenness with God. If my motive of repenting is anything other than being broken it is not true repentance. Once David came to a place of real brokenness, his relationship with God went to a new height. Listen again to his prayer in verse 10; "*create in me a clean heart oh God, renew a loyal spirit within me.*" (emphasis mine). It would be that brokenness and desire to be loyal that would forever change David and cause God to say that David was a man after His heart.

David discovered the secret to an unbroken relationship with God. He clarifies his new understanding in verses 16 and 17, "*You do not desire a sacrifice, or I would offer one. The sacrifice you desire is a broken spirit.*" (emphasis mine). Even in the Old Testament David realizes that God is not interested in the religious offering of bulls and goats. What God wanted was a contrite and broken heart for God Himself. It is no different today. Going to church and Sunday School is a good thing to do. Singing in a choir and attending mid-week prayer services is commendable. But if it does not originate from a broken and contrite heart that yearns for God, then it is just religious sounding of brass, or the tinkling of the cymbal that the writer speaks about in 1 Corinthians 13. It means and counts for nothing.

I made the statement that lack of spiritual nourishment could lead to spiritual death. That no doubt caused some raised eyebrows to some of you reading this chapter. So, although I do not want this book to be a theological discussion I owe it to you the reader to at least back up that statement with Scripture. In 2 Corinthians Paul has written some very straight forward words to the Corinthians regarding what I will refer to as their up and down relationship with God. Then in chapter 7, verse 9 Paul makes this statement, *"the pain caused you to repent and to change your ways. It was the kind of sorrow that God wants His people to have."* Then Paul goes on to say in verse 10, *"There is no regret for that kind of sorrow. But worldly sorrow, which lacks repentance results in <u>spiritual death.</u>"* (emphasis mine). I cannot give you a better definition of brokenness than what is demonstrated here. Until we come to a place where it pains us to be outside the will of God, we can never experience true brokenness in our spirit. It will be within that brokenness that our hunger and thirst for God will arise. It will be within that brokenness that God will rebuild you and your spirit will bear witness with His spirit that you are one with Him. Until our hearts are broken and put into the hands of the Master Carpenter, Jesus, we can never be shaped and molded into what God wants us to be. Then and only then will your hunger be satisfied, and thirst quenched.

If you identify with being hungry and thirsty for more of Him, if you are coming from a place of brokenness, then keep reading.

CHAPTER 2

Seeking God

If you seek me wholeheartedly you will find me. If you look for Me, you will find Me. Jeremiah 29:13

This is not just a promise, it is God crying out, begging you to move past religious routine and seek Him, truly seek Him. It is an invitation to embark on the most rewarding quest you will ever undertake. The quest to seek and find God. The promise of God's presence in our lives is not just some fairytale, it is the cornerstone of why Christ came. I will most likely refer to this passage multiple times throughout this book for the very fact that it is foundational to true Christianity. *"For Christ also once suffered for our sins, the just for the unjust, <u>that He might bring us to God.</u>"* (emphasis mine). (I Peter 3:18 KJV). It is an open declaration, a standing invitation echoing through time. God is not hiding, but waiting, waiting for hearts to turn toward Him, for souls to tune into His frequency, for seekers to earnestly seek Him.

Now, if you believe that God can make a difference in your life today, if you desire something more within your heart and soul, then seek Him! Seek the One who promised to be found! Seeking God is not a one-time event. It is a journey, a continuous walk through the ups and downs of life. It is in the quiet moments of prayer, as well as the loud chaos of the day. In the relationships with those we encounter, God is there, waiting to be found in the multitudes of life's moments.

But remember this, seeking God is not a passive endeavor. It is an active pursuit. It demands dedication, intentionality, and a heart open to transformation. It is about making space for God in the crowded rooms of our minds and hearts. It is about tuning our ears to His voice amid the complexity of life's demands. It is about seeking His will in our decisions, His wisdom in our confusion, and His peace in our turmoil. And in this journey, be reassured of this, *"The Lord's arm is not too weak to save you, nor His ear too deaf to hear you call."* (Isaiah 59:1). He is closer than you think, just waiting to give you the redeeming grace of salvation, and then to spend all eternity listening to the voice of His dear child…you! He is more willing to reveal Himself than you could ever imagine. Just as the dawn dispels the darkness, so does God's presence illuminate the shadows of uncertainty and doubt as it is written in James 4:8, *"Draw near to God and He will draw near to you."* This is the beautiful promise of seeking God.

This journey isn't without its barriers. Distractions are all around us. There are days that the *noise* and *clutter* of life tries to drown out the gentle whisper of God's promise to *"seek and find Me."* I want to challenge you to push past the barriers. Tune out the noise, and in that sacred space of seeking, you will find Him.

The rewards of diligently seeking God are immeasurable. It is not just about finding answers, but discovering a deeper, more intimate relationship with the Creator. It is about aligning your heartbeat with the heartbeat of God himself, about finding peace amidst turmoil, strength in weakness, and hope in despair. The Bible is rich with the stories of seekers such as Abraham, Moses, David, and Mary. These were ordinary people who sought God with extraordinary faith. Their stories are beacons of hope, reminding us that when we seek God with an undivided heart, He reveals himself in ways far beyond our imagination.

Faith will be the compass that guides this journey. It is believing that even when the path is unclear, God is leading. It is trusting that every step taken in seeking Him is a step towards discovering not just more *about* God, but more *of* God.

As we stand on the threshold of this quest, let's take a moment to reflect. Is your heart really tuned to seek God? Are their barriers you need to break? Distractions you need to remove? Make the commitment, here and now to seek God earnestly, relentlessly, passionately. As you read this book, hold on to the promise quoted above that if *"You look for me, you will find me."* Step into this divine assurance with expectation, knowing that when we seek Him wholeheartedly, we are not just on a journey to find God. We are on a journey to discover the depths of His love, the magnitude of His grace, and the absolute certainty of His presence.

I had my first encounter with the Lord in 1966 during a youth church camp at age fifteen. I had no desire at that time to give my life to Christ. There was no conviction of heart that I can recall. My only motive for even being at the camp that year was to get away from a very boring summer in the town to which we had just moved. Well, for those of you who read my last book, Susie had a little something to do with it as well. The point I am trying to make is that up until the moment it happened, I had never given a thought about my need for a Savior. Then, like a lightning bolt from the sky had struck me, I found myself on my knees in an emotional heap. The thought of confessing my sins never entered my mind, I just wanted God in my life.

When I think about it today, God always reminds me about the thief on the cross. Do you realize that he never asked God to forgive his sins? That begs the question, "where in all of Scripture does it say that if you simply say a *sinner's prayer* that you have a free pass to heaven?" The answer to that question is so important we will take an in depth look at that in following chapters.

 When the thief spoke to Christ hanging there next to him, he simply stated, *"Jesus, remember me when you come into your kingdom."* For me, if there was any driving force that night as a young teenage boy, it was simply that I didn't want God to forget me. I didn't want to be left behind, I didn't want to be alone. I wanted Him in my life.

Someone once said, "there is a God-shaped vacuum in our hearts that only God can fill." I now recognize that feeling as being the void that lies within each and every one of us when God is not in our lives. People spend a lifetime trying to fill the void with something, anything that will bring some sense of calm and peace within their heart and soul. Some people seek to fill the void through alcohol or drugs. In my opinion, many clinically diagnosed disorders can be attributed to our seeking to bring a sense of calm, and the filling of that void created by the absence of God in our lives. Some people turn to food to get a sense of being in control of their lives, and the feeling of being full brings a very short-lived feeling of contentment. Others look into a mirror, and they do not like what they see so they rush to the plastic surgeon to change their looks in hopes that a change in appearance will lead to internal changes as well. It would be many years later for me to learn that real change does not come from the outside in. Real change comes from the inside out. And it is not until Christ resides and reigns in our heart and soul that the peace that passes understanding becomes real. It cannot come from anywhere else except the one who created you to be in fellowship with Him.

It would also take another thirteen years before I would understand what was expected of me in order to fill that void. To be as accurate as I can, it was a starry summer night in 1973, sitting on the hood of my car that I came to understand why Jesus could promise paradise to a thief on a cross who never asked for forgiveness or said a sinner's prayer. I was too unworthy to even ask for forgiveness. I was just not worthy enough to be forgiven, I deserved damnation. All I could do was to beg God not to forget me, not to reject me. I would serve Him for the rest of my days if He would just be in my life.

David cried out these words in Psalm 51, *"Have mercy on me, O God, because of your unfailing love, because of Your great compassion, blot out the stain of my sins. Wash me clean from my guilt. Purify me from my sin. For I recognize my rebellion; It haunts me day and night. Against you, and you alone have I sinned; I have done what is evil in your sight. You will be proved right in what You say, and Your judgement against me is just." … "Purify me from my sins, and I will be clean; wash me, and I will be whiter than snow. Oh, give me back my joy again; you have broken me - now let me rejoice. Don't keep looking at my sins. Remove the stain of my guilt. Create a clean heart within me O God. Renew a loyal Spirit within me. Do not banish me from your presence, and don't take Your Holy Spirit from me. Restore to me the joy of your salvation and make me willing to obey You."* That was the cry of my heart in 1973. I would learn many times over how important David's request about obedience would become in order to have that unbroken relationship with God. David was far removed from the will of God when he penned these words in Psalm 51, as was I in 1973. David cried out from a position of brokenness. Broken because He had hurt the heart of God. True repentance comes from a broken heart. Repentance for the sake of escaping hell in not repentance at all.

That was fifty-one years ago that my real journey with God began. I have failed Him many times over these fifty-one years, but I can honestly say, not once has He failed me, and not for a moment has He ever forsaken me. This walk with God has slowly taken me into that deep relationship that God wants for each and every one of us. It is my prayer that *"the peace of God, which surpasses all understanding, will guard your hearts and minds through Christ Jesus our Lord."* (Philippians 4:7 NKJV). Read this passage again slowly. Think what it means to have the Creator of the universe bring perfect peace into your life; to guard your heart and mind from being destroyed by the circumstances of life; to walk so close to God that you recognize His presence not just with you but in you, every minute of every day; to understand, maybe for the first time what Paul meant in 1 Thessalonians 5: 16-18 when he said, *"always be joyful, never stop praying, be thankful in all circumstances, for this is God's will for you who belong to Christ Jesus."* This is what I refer to as an unbroken relationship with God. Is it really possible that I can come to a place in my relationship with Him that He is never out of my thoughts? More importantly, is it possible that I am constantly in His thoughts? Let the journey begin to *"seeking wholeheartedly to find Him."*

Chapter Three

Knowing God

"Who do people say that the Son of Man is?" "Well," they replied, "some say John the Baptist, some say Elijah, and others say Jeremiah or one of the other prophets." Then He asked them, "But who do you say that I am?" Simon Peter answered, "You are the Messiah, the Son of the Living God." Jesus replied, "You are blessed, Simon son of John, because my Father in Heaven has revealed this to you. You did not learn this from any human being." Matthew 16:13-17

Growing up, one of the most spiritual persons in my life was my grandfather. I learned a lot about relational Christianity from him as a little boy. There was one thing that he had a habit of saying that confused me for years. He referred to everyone as brother or sister. It did not matter who they were or how long he had known them. If he was talking to you, he would either recognize you as his brother or his sister. That included my mother and my grandmother. *Grandpa* had discovered that in the spiritual world we are all heirs of God the Father, joint heirs with the Son of God. We were all brothers and sisters for all eternity. He realized that being Christian was relational and not ritual. He had discovered the difference between knowing about God and knowing God. One leads to a routine of religious practice, the other leads to God.

There are four questions that hold the key to understanding God's desire for an unbroken relationship with us.

1)   Why were we created?

In Genesis 4:1 (KJV) the Bible says, *"And Adam knew his wife, Eve."* It is important here to note the Hebrew word for *knew* in this passage. It is the word *yada*, which means the deepest and most intimate knowledge of someone. God's desire is that we know Him in that context. Throughout Scripture He refers to our relationship as Him being the Bridegroom and we are His bride.

When He created Adam and Eve it was a perfect world, a perfect union between Adam and Eve, but most importantly between them and God. That is what He desires of you in your relationship with Him now. The true essence of why Christ came was far more than just the forgiveness of sin. It was to bring us into that *Yada* intimate relationship with God.

To know God, (not just about Him), is to bear His image, and to share in His Kingdom work. God intends for us to glorify Him with the life we live, and to desire to really know Him. We were created to bear His image and His likeness and to live our lives pleasing Him. Paul gives us some insight into why God created us in Colossians 1:16 and 22. *"For through Him, God* *created everything in the heavenly realms, and on earth. He made the things that we see, and the things that we cannot see, such as thrones, kings, and rulers, and authorities in the unseen world. Everything was created through Him <u>and for Him.</u>"* (emphasis mine). Don't gloss over those last few words of that verse. We were created for Him! You are here on this earth for one reason only, God wanted you! God could have chosen to just be content with the birds of the air and the beast of the fields but that wouldn't be enough for God. So, He made you. Not only did He make you, but He made you in the image of Himself. We are the only thing in all of creation that can identify and think like God. Genesis 1:27 tells us that *"God created human beings in his own image; in the image of God he created them."* Being made in His likeness gives us the ability to not just know about Him, but to really know Him, personally and intimately. Therefore, we are drawn to love Him, to worship Him, to serve Him, and most importantly, to have fellowship with Him. Perhaps it is better stated in more modern terms by saying we are created in His likeness so we could relate to Him, to have a relationship with Him that is so strong, that Satan cannot break it or defeat it. This is a relationship that can only be broken by walking outside of His will for you. A relationship broken because of disobedience.

2) What happened when Adam and Eve sinned against God?

The answer is found in Genesis 3:8, *"And they heard the sound of the LORD God walking in the garden in the cool of the day: and Adam and his wife hid themselves from the presence of the LORD God among the trees of the garden."* (KJV). As a result of their disobedience, sin entered the world and the relationship with God was broken. They were now separated from God. The seriousness of that separation is seen in God's reaction to it. He banished them from the garden he had created for them and where He walked in the cool of the day. As if that were not enough, God then stationed an angel in front of the garden with a flaming sword to see that they could not return.

In recent years we have learned a lot about DNA. Physically, our genetic code gets passed down to us by past generations within our families. Everything about us is a result of DNA. From the color of our skin, whether we have curly or straight hair, if we are left-handed or right-handed, it is all determined by our DNA. We also possess spiritual DNA. We inherited that from Adam and Eve. As a result, we know the difference in good and evil. Our spiritual DNA will cause us to justify our actions just as Adam and Eve did. When confronted by God, Eve placed the blame on the serpent using that age old saying, "the devil made me do it." Adam shifted the blame to both Eve and God saying, "That woman that YOU gave me made me do it." (my paraphrase). Thousands of years later we still find ways to justify sin in our lives. It has even found its way into the theology of the church. Listen to just a couple of sayings that have found their way into church doctrine: "We sin every day, in word, thought, and deed." We certainly can't sin in any more ways than that. The problem is that it does not say that in Scripture. That is a quote from theologian Jerome of Stridon, a Catholic priest of the 16th century. Compare that to the words of Christ's own disciple John who stated, *"My dear children, I am writing this to you so that you will NOT (emphasis mine) sin. But if anyone does sin, we have an advocate who pleads our case before the Father. He is Jesus Christ, the one who is truly righteous…. If someone claims, 'I know God,' but doesn't obey God's commandments, that person is a liar and is not living in the truth…. Those who say they live in God should live their lives as Jesus did." (1 John 2:1-6).* Whereas Jerome's commentary is not found in Scripture, John's comments can be found in the Book of First John, chapters two and three. According to John 10:10, Satan seeks to *"steal, kill and destroy"* you and he does this through sin. Now listen to what Jesus says in His own words in the rest of that verse. *"My purpose is to give them a rich and satisfying life."* How does Christ accomplish this? The answer to that is in John 1:29, *"The next day John saw Jesus coming toward him and said, 'Look! The Lamb of God who takes away the sins of the world.'"*

Another saying often made by Christians is that "we are just sinners saved by grace." Now, I believe that most people who make this statement are being sincere and even humble. While it is true that all are sinners who have been saved by grace, it is simply a misrepresentation of who we are as believers. Christ came to take away the sins of the world. We have been set free not in our sin, but free from our sin.

3) So, why did Jesus come?

He came to give you a rich and satisfying life by taking your sins away. But wait, is that the only reason He came? Do you remember that because of Adam and Eve's sin that their relationship with God was broken. Habakkuk 1:13 tells us that God is so Holy that He cannot even look upon sin, much less tolerate it. So, they were banished forever from the Garden. An angel with a flaming sword proclaimed a no trespassing sign. Christ did not come just for the forgiveness of our sins. He came to take away the no trespassing sign and reunite us with God the Father. 1 Peter 3:18 says, "Christ also suffered once for sins, the just for the unjust, *that He might bring us to God.*" Christ's purpose was much more than just the forgiveness of our sins, it was to restore the relationship with God.

Once we understand this, it makes it easier for us to understand a somewhat difficult Scripture found in 1 John 1: 6 and 7, "*So, we are lying if we say that we have fellowship with God but go on living in spiritual darkness; we are not practicing the truth. But if we are living in the light as*

God is in the light, then we have fellowship with each other, and the blood of Jesus, His Son, cleanses us from all sin."

We want to obey Him out of a heart felt love. In fact, our reason for not wanting to sin is that we don't want to hurt His heart. Unfortunately, many church members would tell you they don't want to sin because they do not want to jeopardize missing Heaven. That is a works related approach to salvation rather than a *yada* intimate relationship with God. A validation of a true relationship with God is not wanting to hurt the heart of God.

4) What are the worst words you could ever hear?

Those words are found in Matthew 7:22-23, *"On judgement day many will say to me, 'Lord! Lord! We prophesied in your name and cast out demons in your name and preformed many miracles in your name.' But I will reply, 'I never knew you. Get away from me...'"* Be laser focused on these four words, *"I never knew you!"*

When an author decides to write a book, he or she must first decide on a theme for that book. Then within each chapter there is a key paragraph, and within each paragraph, if he has done a good job, there will be a key sentence. Those four words from the lips of Christ are all these things. It is the most important Christian principle that you must get right. You can sing in the choir every Sunday. You can have a perfect attendance pin for not missing a service in fifty years. You can give your tithe and teach Sunday school. You can prophesy and even cast out demons in the name of Jesus, and still hear those words, *"I never knew you."*

Right now, I am wishing this was an audio book so that you could hear the emphasis and tone Jesus was using here. Being a true Christian is not about what you do, it is about who you know. If you never spend time in His Word, if you never spend time in prayer, if His Spirit is not alive within the depths of your soul guiding you and teaching you, you simply do not know God. Once again, let me emphasize that there is a vast difference in knowing *about* God and in truly *knowing* God. The first is a religious experience that will lead you nowhere, the other is a relationship with God the Father that leads to a joyous and fulfilled eternal life starting now.

Chapter Four

It's About Relationship

Christ also suffered for sin once, the righteous for the unrighteous, that He might bring us to God." 1 Peter 3:18

Christ purpose was not only forgiveness of sin but to bring us back to an unbroken relationship with God. As a point of clarity, I am not talking about your salvation at this point. I am focusing on what comes after salvation. The most important thing that matters to God is the relationship He shares with us. In the book of Genesis, we find that God would come to the garden in the cool of the day to walk with Adam. Once sin entered the picture, we do not see that God ever walked in the garden again. In fact, He banished Adam and Eve from the garden and put a flaming sword to keep them from re-entering. That is when the relationship between God and mankind was broken. When Christ came it was not just for the purpose of forgiving our sins but to restore that relationship with God the Father. 1 Peter 3:18 tells us that *"For Christ also suffered once for sins, the righteous for the unrighteous, that he might **bring us to God."*** (emphasis mine).

When we live in an unbroken relationship with the Father, we begin to understand His heart and His very nature. We get to the place that our love for God gets greater and greater as a result of that unbroken relationship. Jesus asked the question of the disciples *"do you love me?"* He never asked them *"are you saved?"* When we truly repent and ask God into our heart He gifts us with forgiveness of those sins. That is the beginning of a new relationship. Think of it like a wedding ceremony. We say, "I do" and we are pronounced man and wife. The couple does not leave that ceremony and go their separate ways. They live a life together and everything else in their lives takes a backseat to that new relationship that they committed to. Spiritually, saying "I do" is where we ask God into our lives and sin is forgiven. At this point we live the rest of our lives together in unbroken faithful relationship to Him.

Matthew 7:13 and 14 says, *"You can enter God's Kingdom only through the narrow gate. The highway to hell is broad ,and its gate is wide for the many who choose that way. But the gateway to life is very narrow, and the road is difficult, and only a few ever find it."* (emphasis mine). The church in North America has been so focused on the forgiveness of sin, we have forgotten that there is a road to be walked, and few ever find it. True repentance compels us to walk that road.

Listen to the words of God Himself through the prophet Hosea in chapter 6 verse 3 and again in verse 6. *"Oh, that we might know the Lord! Let us press on to know Him. He will respond to us as surely as the arrival of dawn or the coming of rains in early spring ... I want you to show love, not offer sacrifices. I want you to know me more than I want burnt offerings."* God expresses His desire for us to know Him. It is important once again to note here that He does not say that He wants us to know about Him, He wants us to know Him. You must be walking down that narrow road to know Him. Repentance gives us forgiveness of our sins, but it is the walking down the road with Him by our side that we begin to understand His nature. It is in that walk that we begin to understand the mind of God.

Matthew told us that sometimes the road is difficult and as a result few ever find it. When tragedy comes our way, if we do not know the heart of God, we struggle with the *why* tragedies happen in our life. I counseled with a young husband and father who had lost his job. He had repented of sin and asked Christ to come into his heart several years before. He asked me, *"Why did God let this happen to me? I pay my tithe, I am in church every Sunday, it just seems like God has it in for me."* He had done what his church taught him to do. He said the sinner's prayer, asked Jesus into his heart, and then he was *saved*. He found a good church, went through the membership class, learned the doctrine of the church, and even sacrificed part of his paycheck by tithing. He started down the road of understanding church, but that is not the narrow road of knowing God. When faced with difficulty, he had no assurance that God had a plan and purpose. Instead, he concluded that God must have it *in* for him. Read what God said through Hosea again. *"I want you to know me more than I want burnt offerings."* (Hosea 6:6). Burnt offerings were the religious practice of the day. Today it is attending church, paying tithe, and even singing in the choir. We can practice those things all our life and still not know God. Those things are not bad, as a matter of fact they are good, but God is saying that He wants us to know Him more than He wants those things. Let me clarify again. I am not talking about gaining knowledge about God. What He wants is an intimate, personal relationship where His heart becomes our heart. Until you begin to walk down the road of knowing God you are stuck with a religious ritual walk that will not sustain you when the difficult times of life occur.

I want to take a moment here to say more about tragedies in life. It is too important to just make a statement that says if we are in an unbroken relationship that some tragedies won't break our hearts, or that we won't ask God why. As I write this tonight, I have been reminded that seven years ago my wife and I lost not one, but both of our sons. I have watched as the pain at times has overwhelmed my wife. There are those days that it is all she could do just to have a somewhat normal day. No amount of time or space will ever cause her to miss them any less after all these years than she did in the days and weeks that followed those dark days. What does make the difference is to know that the day will come when the walks in the garden with God will return. The day when we will know as we are known. The lonely days will be gone. The emptiness of a mother's heart will be removed. Quite frankly I do not know how those who do not trust in God survive such a loss. If there is no God, there is no hope. If for no other reason to want to know God, this one alone would be enough for me. All tears wiped away, all pain will be gone, and life will be restored as God had originally intended.

Acts 13:22 says, *"But God removed Saul and replaced him with David, a man about whom God said, 'I have found David son of Jesse, a man after my own heart. He will do everything I want him to do.'"* God acknowledges here that David sought the heart of God. He did not say that David lived a perfect life. We are talking about a man who committed adultery and then had the woman's husband killed to cover it up. If that had happened today, David's face would be all over the news. Television stations would devote countless hours covering the story. Millions of people would be glued to their televisions following the trial. Nancy Grace would be there every evening telling us why he was guilty and that he deserved no less than the death penalty. This is the man that God said, *"he is a man after my own heart."* So, what changed in David that would cause God to make such a statement about him?

Part of the answer is found in the verse we just read. *"He will do everything I want him to do."* This is where the journey to what I refer to as an unbroken relationship begins. It is called obedience. David found favor with God first because God recognized David was willing to be obedient about the things of God. I could write a chapter detailing all the times I have been challenged for my emphasis on obedience. Many believe that if we emphasize obedience that somehow it nullifies the fact that we are saved by grace and not of works. It totally disregards such Scriptures as John 14:15, *"If you love me, keep my commandments.* "I have been told that to focus on obedience leads to legalism. Paul says in Acts 13:22 that it leads to the heart of God.

That brings us to the heart of what it takes to have an unbroken relationship – that is loving God. Love is a word that has been so overused and abused that it has lost its true meaning. As we take that walk down the narrow path we begin to discover things about Him. We start to realize that even when bad things come our way, He is there with us. Our knowledge about God, turns into knowledge of God. Until we reach that point in our relationship, we cannot truly love God. When the love comes alive, we are well on our way to the path that leads to an unbroken relationship.

David could now pen these words that he wrote in Psalms 27:4, *"The one thing I ask of the Lord, the thing that I seek most, is to live in the house of the Lord all the days of my life delighting in the Lord's perfections and meditating in His Temple."* According to Webster's dictionary the word *live* means to make my home in a particular place or with a particular person. In David's case it meant both. It is said that *"home is where the heart is."* David has come to the place that more than anything else, he wanted both his home and his heart to dwell with God for ever. He delighted in the things God did. The King James Version of the Bible uses the word *gaze*. Think of when you fell in love with your soulmate. If you were like me, you looked upon the love of your life with amazement. I saw her in everything I did, and everywhere I went. Her image was forever burned into my subconscious mind. So, it now was with David. He saw God in everything he did and everywhere he went. To meditate, meant to think upon the things of God rather than the things of the world.

David found the key that opened the door to a beautiful and unbroken relationship with God the Father. So, I have questions for you. Are you desiring God's presence? Are you satisfied with just the forgiveness of sin, or do you want more? Are you settling for less than what God can do for you and through you? Are you settling for what God can do for you rather than what He can do in you? Christ came both to forgive our sins, and to restore our relationship with God the Father. Until both happen, your journey is incomplete.

Chapter Five

Living in The Unbroken Relationship

"I thank my God always for you because of the grace of God which was given you in Christ Jesus so that in **everything you were enriched** *in Him, in* **all speech**, *[empowered by the spiritual gifts] and in* **all knowledge** *[with insight into the faith]. In this way our testimony about Christ was confirmed and established in you, so that* **you are not lacking in any spiritual gift** *[which comes from the Holy Spirit], as you eagerly wait [with confident trust] for the revelation of our Lord Jesus Christ [when He returns]. And He will also confirm you to the end [keeping you strong and free of any accusation, so that you will be blameless and beyond reproach in the day of the return of our Lord Jesus Christ].* **God is faithful, He is reliable, trustworthy and ever true** *to His promise.* **He can be depended on**, *and through Him you were called into fellowship with His Son, Jesus Christ our Lord."* (emphasis mine) Corinthians 1:4-9 (AMB)

To understand the importance of this passage of Scripture we have to look at the condition that existed in the church in Corinth. Corinth was a city much like many of our cities today. It had lost its moral compass. Immorality ruled the city. Sexual perversion was common practice. There was little sense of right and wrong. People would take their neighbor to court, willing to lie and slander to make a profit. Unfortunately, the church in Corinth reflected the society in which it lived. You could not tell the difference in the character of those within the church from those outside the church. Members fighting against one another, suing other members. Sexual immorality and a host of other sins were commonplace and accepted practice inside the four walls of the church.

With this in mind, let me now ask a thought-provoking question. Is the best Christ has to offer us a life of striving, stumbling, repenting, and repeating much like the Corinthian Church? Is that what we see in Scripture? When we first came to Christ most of us had a deep sense of freedom and there was a joy that could only come from God. Then the cares of the world began to set in. Our victorious living wasn't so victorious anymore. For some reason, church didn't seem to hold all the answers. We surrendered our victorious living to a life of striving, stumbling, repenting when our faith fails us, and then repeating the process all over again. We bought into the belief that total victory and living a Godly life isn't possible. After all, we are just human.

The most accurate word I can use to describe this lifestyle is deception. We start acting on something that quite honestly just isn't true. The result is we start accepting far less in our spiritual walk than what God intended for us. What I see happening in so many churches today is that there are no Joshua's and Caleb's anymore. In Numbers chapters 13 and 14 we find the story of God sending twelve spies into the

Promised Land to see what they would be up against to take possession of the land. Ten of those twelve came back and reported that it would be impossible for Israel to defeat the giants that lived there. They might as well give up now. It was simply not possible to overcome the enemy. Only Joshua and Caleb believed God was big enough to bring total victory and in turn fulfill the promise He made that they would inherit the land. Thank God for those two faithful men of God. Had it not been for them, church history would look much different today. We need more Joshua's and Caleb's within the body of Christ that have a different perspective than the status quo. Christians who believe God can bring complete victory over *"every sin that so easily besets us"* (Hebrews 12:1). Those who believe we can walk in the fullness and the power of God Almighty. Paul is making it very clear that God has made available everything we need to live a Godly life. Many theologians focus on the statement that we will be blameless on the day of His return. But there is so much more to this passage. He will keep you strong in this life until that day comes. Read how Peter further makes his case for the power of the believer in 2 Peter 1:3. *"His divine power has given us everything we need for a Godly life through our knowledge of Him who called us by His own glory and goodness."* Again, I call your attention to the wording here. Peter says that we are to have knowledge *of* Him, and not simply *about* Him. There is a huge difference in the meaning of those two words. The more I know of Him in a personal way, the easier it is to realize His divine power is enough for me to live a Godly life. But it doesn't end there! Look at what Peter says next in verse four of that same chapter. *"Through these He has given us His very great and precious promises, so that through them you may participate in His divine nature, having escaped the corruption in the world caused by evil desires."* This is power in the life of the believer. Power to rise above the mediocre, anemic life that most believers are trapped in. He has given us His divine nature to not just live in us but to thrive in us. He has given it for the purpose of us escaping the corruption and evil of this world. As Jesus Himself said in John 8:36, *"So, if the Son sets you free, you are truly free!"* He certainly is not saying that we are free to live a weak faithless life. We are not free to just strive, stumble, repent, and repeat it again and again until this life is over. We have been set free to live within the divine nature of a Holy God and possess the power to overcome the world.

Paul continues to explain the deeper purpose of Christ's coming in Galatians 4. Read carefully to the following verses: *"God sent His Son …that we might receive adoption as His sons. And because you are sons, God has sent forth the Spirit of His Son into your hearts,* (emphasis mine) *crying out 'Abba Father.' Therefore, you are no longer a slave but a son, and if a son, then an heir of God through Christ."* (v. 5-7)… *But now after you have known God, or rather are known by God, how is it that you turn again to the weak and beggarly elements to which you desire again to be in bondage?"(v. 9 NKJV).* You are far more than a struggling *sinner saved by grace!* You are a son or daughter of the living God, joint heir with Jesus Christ! The Spirit of Christ lives in your heart, available twenty-four hours a day to give you everything you need to overcome this world, to live by His power not only to overcome sin, but to fulfill whatever He ask of you to do in serving Him. Paul admonished them to not live weak and beggarly lives. It is a deception born of Satan to believe that I cannot live a completely victorious life in Christ. I feel it necessary to quote God from the Old Testament to understand that God has always required obedience and a life above sin. *"You shall be holy, for I the Lord your God am holy."* (Leviticus 19:2b). The Hebrew word here for holy is *qadash* which means to be separated from the world and worldliness. Again, it is a deception born of Satan to believe that I must settle for anything less than complete and total victory through Christ. God is making it very clear that His people can and are expected to live holy lives. Some will say that this was the Old Testament, and we are now under grace. This is true, but God's nature has never changed. In the last book of the Old Testament God makes this statement found in Malachi 3:6. *"For I am the Lord, I do not change."* His demand that we live holy lives has not changed.

Christ has made it possible for us to rise above our spiritual weakness. To live in all the fullness of God. To have complete knowledge of God even to the point of being His voice here on earth. To be full partners with His Son Christ Jesus. God is faithful. God is reliable. God is trustworthy. God is ever true. God can be depended on.

Hopefully, we are making the case that Christ came for far more than just to forgive our sins. He came to bring us to God. He came to live within our heart and soul. He came to give us the ability to live joyful, powerful, victorious lives, far from a life of striving, stumbling, repenting, and repeating.

Chapter Six

The Pearl of Great Price

The Kingdom of Heaven is like a treasure that a man discovered hidden in a field. In his excitement, he hid it again and sold everything he owned to get enough money to buy the field. Again, the Kingdom of Heaven is like a merchant on the lookout for choice pearls. When he discovered a pearl of great value, he sold everything he owned and bought it! Matthew 13:44-46

What is it that you value more than anything else in life? This is another important question that you must answer if you want to enter into an unbroken relationship with God the Father. It is really very easy to determine what you value in life. Just inventory the following things: Where is the majority of your time spent in a normal twenty-four hour period? Is the money you invest in the stock market or elsewhere matched by what you invest in God's Kingdom? Which excites you more, your favorite ball team winning the game, or a soul that just surrendered their life to Christ?

When my children were growing up, they would ask me, "Daddy, if you had all the money in the world what would you do with it?" I confess that I enjoyed daydreaming about what I would do with that kind of money. I found myself being a very charitable person. Building beautiful homes for my children, new cars for the grandkids, vacation homes scattered abroad for myself. You get the picture. Now that I am old, I have come to realize that there is absolutely no value in the material things of life. Once I am gone, everyone will divide up everything I leave behind and life will go on for them a little while longer, but not forever. They too will someday realize that the material things will lose their shine and once again those things will be left behind.

The point Christ was making really has nothing to do with the material aspect of the parable. There are two messages in these verses. First, they had the ability to know and understand the value of what they had found. Secondly, once they had discovered it, they would not allow themselves to be denied obtaining it. Nothing else mattered. They would not be satisfied any longer with the material things they had acquired thus far in life. All that mattered now was possessing that Pearl of Great Price.

Many Christians today have either forgotten the value of a relationship with God, or after years of what I have referred to as striving, stumbling, repenting, and repeating, they settle for something less in their spiritual lives. I have spent many years walking with the Lord for years. I have been more than an occasional reader of His Word. I have spent more than a few minutes most days in prayer. I have witnessed great and mighty things the Lord has done throughout my life. Yet only in the last two years have I come to realize the true value of an unbroken relationship with our Heavenly Father.

I just stated that there were two messages in these passages of Scripture. There is actually a third. It is that God, the one who created you, sees you as the Pearl of Great Price! God recognizes that you have so much value that He gave His greatest treasure, His own Son to purchase you. When you really understand the value that God places upon you, it should not be a stretch to see that God would not only pay the price of His Son, but that He would use everything at His disposal to keep the Pearl, you, in pristine shape at all times.

 Growing up, my father taught me the importance of taking care of things so that they would not lose their value. He was just as adamant about things I borrowed. I can hear him saying right now, "Son, if you ever borrow something, you return it in better shape than when you borrowed it." Isn't it true that we care for the things that are important to us.

Years ago, I owned an old pickup truck that I used mainly for camping and fishing. It wasn't much to look at, but I really loved and cared for it. At the time I was the only one among our family and friends that owned a truck at all. I can assure you that everyone knew I was meticulous about my vehicles. I washed that old truck almost every weekend. I kept the oil changed and made sure it stayed in mechanical good condition. When it came to paying the insurance, I would get the best coverage I could possibly buy for it. Nothing but the very best was good enough as far as I was concerned. Even my insurance agent would try and get me just to take the minimum to keep it on the road. I followed my father's advice to a fault.

Eventually I began to recognize a growing problem. Being the only one in my circle who owned a truck, I found others using it more than me. I was doing the upkeep and paying the insurance so everyone else but me could use it. In addition, most times when it was returned I would have to clean it up, refill the gas tank, and sometimes I would discover some new scratch or dent that was not there before. It all came crashing down one weekend when my boss at the time wanted to borrow it for some yard work. He only lived around the corner and promised to have it back in a couple of hours. That turned into two days and when he did return it, instead of parking it in my driveway he parked it on the curb at the side of our house. I thought that was odd, but didn't really think much of it. I let it sit there over the weekend and then went to move it. I started it up and put it in gear, but it didn't move. The forward gears had been stripped out of it. The only direction it would go was in reverse. Now, I knew why he parked it on the curb. He drove it all the way from his house to mine in reverse but couldn't drive it into the driveway. The discouraging part was that he did not care enough to even tell me about it. No apology, no offer to explain what happened, nothing. He had gotten out of it what he needed and saw no need to say or do anything. As much as I loved my truck, I had it fixed and sold it. Needless to say, my respect for my boss was lost as well. The problem was that he did not see the same value in it that I had seen. It was just an easy way for him to get the job done.

Many *Christians* approach their relationship with Christ in much the same way. It is the way to avoid hell, or to go to heaven but they put little or no investment into taking care of the relationship. They do not see the value of the Pearl of Great Price.

The Apostle Paul made a very profound statement in Philippians 3:14 when he said, *"I press on toward the prize of the high calling of Christ Jesus my Lord."* He knew and understood what that prize was. There is a pattern to most of Paul's writings in the New Testament. He usually starts out talking about what Christ has done for us, then follows it by addressing what our response to those things should be. Nowhere is this more prevalent than in the book of Romans. In the first eleven chapters Paul talks about what Christ has done for us, the fact that salvation is for everyone, that we can have victory over sin, the free gift of eternal life, no condemnation, and most importantly, the days of striving and stumbling can be put behind us. I am praying that you are beginning to see the value of the relationship God is offering you.

Paul changes course in chapter twelve. From there through the end of the book he speaks to what our response should be. In essence, his message is about how we take care of the relationship so that it becomes unbroken.

Read carefully what Paul says in Romans 12:1 and 2, *"I beseech you therefore brethren, by the mercies of God, that you present your bodies a living sacrifice, holy, acceptable unto God, <u>which is your reasonable service</u> (emphasis mine). And be not conformed to this world but be transformed by the renewing of your mind, that you may prove what is that good, and acceptable, and perfect will of God."*

Paul is instructing us not to conform to the world. Conformity to this world is a powerful thing. It is extremely difficult not to conform when that is where the majority of the world is. The Greek word here for *conformed* means to follow the same pattern, or to be in union with. To be in union with the world is the same as being in union with the devil. Instead, we are to be transformed. But how does that happen? Only by the renewing of your mind. It is not about what you do as Christian. It is about who you are. When all we do is to conform to religious routine and rituals, but our minds have not been renewed, we are missing the relationship. We have already discussed the dangers of that when we looked at Matthew 7:23 (KJV) where Jesus told some religious people *"I never knew you, depart from me."* In the end, all that matters is the relationship, not the works that I do.

When as Christians our minds are transformed, we no longer think like we used to think. We think differently as believers than we did when we were sinners. Our morals as a sinner sharply contrast with our morals as a Christian. The things we once detested when we were sinners, we now embrace and enjoy as believers. Those things we once enjoyed as sinners, we now regret we ever did. All of this gives evidence to the fact that we are being transformed and that our minds are being renewed. This is what brings us ever closer to an unbroken relationship that God desires to have with us.

Read Paul's words in Philippians 2:7 *"He stripped Himself [of all privileges and rightful dignity], so as to assume the guise of a servant (slave) in that he became like men and was born a human being."* (AMPC). He left His home in glory, stripped Himself of His rightful place with God, and endured the cross all because He wanted a relationship with you. Do you see the value yet? It is not just about the forgiveness of sin that has to happen, which certainly you have to ask for, but He also came to restore us to an unbroken relationship with God the Father.

Doing things for God will never lead to fulfillment simply because you never sellout. If we are not careful, doing things for God, although admirable, can be about performance not relationship. You check the box and chalk it up to being right with God. There is a word for that, it is called legalism. Whenever our relationship with God is either knowledge based, or performance based, it never puts us in a position to forsake all. But when you do what you do because of the relationship, you will go farther with God than you have ever been before. You will be entering the unbroken relationship that God desires to have with you.

The Hidden Treasure - the Pearl of Great Price, is the relationship we can have with Him. When Jesus was here on earth, His offer to the twelve disciples was *follow me*. After the cross and after the resurrection, the message became, *"abide in Me."* It changed their relationship with Him so much that they were willing to die for Him. This is what is meant by an unbroken relationship.

I have stated it before in this book and have no doubt I will say it many more times, Christ did not come for the purpose of us going to heaven. That is what some would call the icing on the cake. He came to restore us to an unbroken relationship with God the Father.

Let me end this chapter with a modern-day parable shared with me by a friend. It helps to bring clarity to what we are talking about. A man and woman marry and the only thing keeping either the man or woman from having an extra-marital affair is the thought of being discovered and the high price that he or she would pay. They could lose their family and have to leave their home. It could cost them their reputation in the community. A divorce would bring shame or a sense of failure, not to mention child support or alimony. The fear of those things is what prevents them from having an affair. So, they do what married couples are supposed to do and they stayed married. That is a sad commentary to why they would stay faithful to one another.

On the other hand, in the home across the street there is another man and woman who are married. The only thing keeping either him or her from having an affair is their loving, caring relationship for one another. They refuse to do anything that would hurt the heart of their spouse. Identify the spouse you would like your husband or wife to be like. Is it the one who did what they were supposed to do to stay out of trouble, or the spouse who did what they did based on a loving relationship?

It becomes obvious concerning God and us. It is about relationship. It is not about doing what we are supposed to do.

The things we do for God will be driven by performance or by relationship. Which do you think He would prefer?

Chapter Seven

Living The New Life

Since you have been raised to new life with Christ, set your sights on the realities of heaven. Colossians 3:1

The Scripture below is so foundational to having an unbroken relationship with God that I want to challenge you before reading this chapter to do something. Simply read these verses several times and ask God to reveal the meaning of them to you. Take your time. Meditate and pray about what Paul is saying. Ask the Holy Spirit to speak the truth and power of the passage into your heart and mind. You will be well on your way to that unbroken relationship with God once you capture the depth of Paul's words.

"Since you have been raised to new life with Christ, set your sights on the realities of heaven, where Christ sits in the place of honor at God's right hand. Think about the things of heaven, not the things of earth. For you died to this life and your real life is hidden with Christ in God. And when Christ, who is your life, is revealed to the whole world, you will share in all his glory.

So put to death the sinful, earthly things lurking within you. Have nothing to do with sexual immorality, impurity, lust, and evil desires. Don't be greedy, for a greedy person is an idolator, worshipping the things of this world. Because of these sins the anger of God is coming. You used to do these things when your life was still a part of this world. But now is the time to get rid of anger, rage, malicious behavior, slander, and dirty language. Don't lie to each other, for you have stripped off your old sinful nature and all its wicked deeds. Put on your new nature and be renewed as you get to know your Creator and become like Him. In this new life it doesn't matter if you are Jew or Gentile, circumcised or uncircumcised, barbaric, uncivilized, slave or free. Christ is all that matters, and he lives in all of us!" (Colossians 3:1-11).

The world that we live in today is more broken and sin-filled than at any other time in my seventy-two years. I see people every day that have fallen victim in one way or another to the pathetic life this world has to offer. The results of a world that allows every sin imaginable to rule people's lives is tearing apart the very soul of mankind. A world where there is a growing rejection of the very existence of God leaves us without hope, only despair. The results of a world that has rejected God are all around us. Our cities are no longer safe to live in. I grew up in a world where Christ was still a cornerstone in most families. We left our homes unlocked at night as we slept without the fear of a home invasion. Our automobiles would be parked in open driveways with the keys left in the ignition. Christians could openly talk about their faith in God without fear of being hated for it.

Then, slowly and subtlety we began to push God out of our communities. Children could no longer start their school day with prayer. To care about the soul of our friends and neighbors is now met with anger and rejection. To continue to believe in God labels a person as weak, needing some sort of crutch to lean on. I could give you a timeline of society removing God from the very world He created but that is not the point I want to make here. What is more important is the impact that a godless culture has on our society.

Without God to cast our cares upon creates a void that needs to be filled with something else. Alcohol and drug addiction is tearing apart the very fabric of society. It is no longer safe to send your children to many public schools for fear of being shot, or pulled into the drug scene by those wishing to make you *need* what they are selling. Others seek to fill the godless void in their soul by going from one sexual liaison to another but never finding fulfillment. The Bible tells us that we can have a *peace that passes understanding, a peace that the world cannot provide.* That too has been replaced by taking a pill to *calm the nerves.* To summarize, at best we are living in a pathetic, broken, and sin-filled world where for most God no longer lives within the heart and soul.

The good news is that if our relationship with God is right, then we find that our life in this sadly sinful life can be overcome. There is nothing that will overwhelm you. Nothing will defeat you. You will not be destroyed by the circumstances that life brings. Tragedies will still come. Heartache will still exist, but it will not destroy you.

I opened this chapter by asking you take some time to think about what Paul had been trying to communicate in Colossians 3:1-11. Let me go back and break out what I was praying you would see.

Raised to new life.

If you have truly sought God for the forgiveness of sin and committed to living an obedient life according to Scriptures, then you have been raised to a new life and a new way of living. That new life and new way of living is the relationship with God, the Creator of your soul. We need to move away from the mindset that on a certain day and time my sins were forgiven and that is all there is. Back in the 1970's there was a picture that became popular for sale in bookstores. It was a picture of a cross that lay as a bridge across a deep crevice. Below the bridge was a vast lake of fire and on the other side of the bridge people were being escorted into heaven. That picture had a powerful message behind it, and I have no doubt has helped bring souls into God's Kingdom. But it misses the mark of why the cross was so vital. On the other side of that bridge that the cross creates, is God himself waiting with open arms to begin a spiritual courtship between us and Him. We have been taught that the forgiveness of sin is what allows us entrance into Heaven, but a study of Scripture lets us know that this misses the real purpose of the cross which was to bring us back into relationship with God. Our focus should go well beyond the forgiveness of sin and realize that God is waiting on us to live in the fullness of His Spirit. Plainly stated, the purpose of the cross is not just the forgiveness of sin. The purpose is an unbroken relationship with our Creator. The Apostle Paul says it this way in writing to the church at Corinth, *"Therefore, if any man be in Christ, he is a new creature: old things are passed away; behold, all things are become new."* (2 Corinthians 5:17 KJV). I do not want this book to become a subject of theological debate, but I earnestly desire for you to live in absolutely everything God has provided for you. Being raised to a new life means my old life is gone. I have a new way of thinking, a new way of acting. I literally become a new creature. It is not a cleaned-up version of my old self but rather a new person altogether, a new mind, a new heart, and a new Spirit. Paul is clearly stating that *"old things have passed away, ALL* (emphasis mine) *things have become new."*

Set your sights on the things of heaven

You couldn't tell it by looking at me now, but I ran track when I was in junior high school. The combination of age as well and too many carbohydrates in my diet have changed a youthful, slender young boy into a somewhat plump old man! There were a variety of races our track team ran such as the 100-yard dash, the 220, 440, or the mile. My specialty was the 440 and before I was in the ninth grade I set the Junior High record for the fastest time in our school. That led to a showdown with the Senior High record holder and me for the fastest overall time in the school. The race was set during the school lunch hour so that the student body could attend the big race. I was mentally prepared, and I had confidence that I could outrun my opponent. My time was actually almost a second faster than his in practice. All I needed to do was just to stay focused and I could beat this senior and claim the honor as the fastest runner in school history. I heard the starter gun fire, and the race was on. I would stay with him for the first quarter of the race so that he knew I was a serious threat. Then I faded back into the middle of the runners and paced myself for the finish. We got to the back turn, and I made my move. He couldn't see me behind him without breaking stride just enough to turn around to see if he could spot me among the other runners. My tactic was clear, his turning around would slow him down just a fraction of a second. I was gaining on him, and I can hear my coach and students cheering me on. I stayed laser focused on my opponent and as we came around the final turn, I caught up with him. Side by side we both turned on the afterburners using every ounce of energy we have left. Finally, I passed him and collapse to the ground at what I thought was the finish line. The problem was I was five yards short of the real goal line. My focus was all wrong in the end. I was focused on my opponent when I should have been focused on the finish line.

What does this have anything to do with the reality of heaven? In having an unbroken relationship with God, it has everything to do with it. If our goal is to focus on *doing* all the right things (mechanics) such as attending church, Sunday School, tithing, we risk falling short of the finish line. I am not telling you those things are not important because they are. Paul recognized this problem when writing to the Colossians. When I focus on the *what* I fall into thinking of what I *do* rather than the *why* behind it. If the goal is an unbroken relationship with God, the focus must be the reality of what Christ did. Look to heaven where He is seated at the right hand of the Father. That is the finish line. Do not fall five yards short!

Running the race that day was difficult. My muscles grew tired. My legs were cramping up, and I became dizzy and disoriented.

This life we live here on earth is far more difficult than my race. We face disappointments, heartaches, tragedies, and disease. We will fall short of the finish line when these things come upon us. We become spiritually fatigued. Our faith falls short. We become spiritually disoriented and ask *why*! Focus on the real finish line which is Christ seated at the right hand of the Father.

Paul goes on to tell us to think on the things of heaven and not the things of this world. This is so essential to an unbroken relationship with God, as well as the peace that it brings. Yet, it may be the greatest obstacle we fail to overcome that keeps us from achieving the fullness of peace that an unbroken relationship offers to us as believers.

I heard someone make the statement one time, "you are so worldly minded that you are not any heavenly good." I have always understood this as a lighthearted reminder not to want the *things* this world offers such as expensive cars, big houses, jewelry, or designer clothing. That list could get quite long if we just thought about it for just a few minutes.

While the above is very true and most believers struggle with at least one or more of those areas, I believe that the writer understood, that when our focus is on the things in this life, we will never walk in the fullness of what God has to offer us.

How is it that God equips us to have His thoughts and not our thoughts? How is it that His ways become our ways? When we are born into this world, we are born with a set of five senses: sight, hearing, taste, touch, and smell. When we are born again, we are born with a spiritual set of senses. His Spirit begins to bear witness with our Spirit. Things that used to not bother us begin to matter because of our new birth. When we learn to relate to God spirit to Spirit, over time we learn how to trust our spirit over our thoughts. We learn to hear that still small voice, to sense God's direction for our lives, and to have faith, even in the darkest of nights, that God is with us. This gives so much clarity to how God could say to those who prophesized in His name, and even healed in His name, "I never knew you, depart from me." It is all about the relationship, no more, no less.

Early in my Christian walk I was taught that the mark of a good Christian was measured by the things one did. It was essential that a Christian would attend church every Sunday morning and again on Sunday evening. If you wanted to be among the spiritually elite, you would need to attend mid-week prayer service as well. You used your *talents* in service to the Lord. Some sang in the choir, others taught Sunday School. If you were truly faithful you became a soul winner for Jesus. The more of these things you could check off the list meant the more of God's approval you would receive. This became so ingrained within me that I thought any failure to do these things put my very soul in danger.

Let me be very clear here. I am not telling you that you should not do these things. What I am saying is that you cannot measure your standing with God by the things you do. Keep in mind that Jesus' illustration of judgement day addressed the very heart of how God looks at your relationship with Him. These were *religious* people standing before him; people who had testified of God, prophesied in His name, even healed people in His name and yet they heard the most awful words anyone will ever hear, *"I never knew you, depart from me."* I cannot over emphasize this. It is not about what you do; it is about having a personal intimate relationship with the One who created you.

Understanding Jesus' illustration of judgement day is central to the message of the entire New Testament. If I fail to properly communicate this, then this book will have been written in vain. More important will be that you will have missed the real reason why Jesus gave His life on the cross. I can envision the judgement day scene that draws those dreadful words *"I never knew you"* sounding something like this, "Lord, I was in church every Sunday, I gave above my tithe to help with the building fund, what do you mean you don't know me?" Jesus replies, *"I never knew you to:*

> • *Spend time in prayer with me. The only times you prayed to me is when you needed something.*
>
> • *I never knew you to just want to spend time with me.*
>
> • *I never knew you to spend time reading the letters (the Bible) I wrote to you.*
>
> • *I never knew you to obey the things I asked you to do.*
>
> • *I know a lot about the things you did, but I never knew you. Most of all, you never got to know me."*

The typical person who calls themselves Christian today:

- Has some (not much) knowledge about God instead of intimate knowledge of God.
- Prays (not much) to ask God for things rather than simply talking with Him.

The key to an unbroken relationship with God is to begin to understand His every thought and motive regarding you and your life in Him. We must get to the place where our love for God is greater because of that unbroken relationship. Jesus asks, *"do you love me?"* Not are you saved yet. He didn't come just to forgive our sins but to bring us back into relationship with God the Father.

Chapter Eight

Growing in God

Christ also suffered once for our sins, the just for the unjust, that He may bring us to God. 1 Peter 3:18

It is important to note in the above verse that Peter does not say to bring us to *heaven*, but rather Christ's purpose was to bring us to *God.* Knowing God is the cornerstone of the Christian life. As we have said, there is a big difference in having knowledge about God and knowing God. Mark 1:23 and 24 tells the story of a man possessed by an evil spirit. When Jesus arrives at the scene the evil spirit asked the question, *"have you come to destroy us? We know who you are, the Holy One of God."* (emphasis mine). They knew who God was, and most likely had more knowledge of Him than the average Christian possess today. But the demon was still a demon. His knowledge about God did not change his demon nature. I have talked with many people who thought they were Christians because of their vast knowledge about the God of the Bible. Many of them attend church regularly, were in Bible studies, and even loved to talk about Scripture. But knowledge about God does not equal knowing God. John 17:3 says, *"And this is eternal life, and that they may know You, the only true God, and Jesus Christ whom You have sent."* John is clearly stating that eternal life comes from knowing God. It is not about a *sinner's prayer;* it is not about how much I know. It is about who I know. Knowing God in an intimate personal relationship of faith and trust is what brings us eternal life. It is the cornerstone of the Christian life.

Christ did not come just to forgive our sins. Neither did He come so that we could go to heaven, or to escape hell. His purpose in coming was to restore our relationship with God the Father. You cannot have a relationship that is solely based on knowledge.

A marriage relationship is a perfect example. You can know your spouse's name, date of birth, the color of their hair, who their parents are, their height, what foods they like. But until you hold them in your arms, look deep into their eyes, have that first kiss, it is all just knowledge. God is not interested in our knowledge about Him. He wants one thing only… that one thing is you!

1 John 4:16 gives more evidence of God's love and desire for relationship. *"We know how much God loves us, and we have put our trust in that love. God is love, and all who live in love live in God, and God lives in them. And as we live in God, our love grows more perfect."* A sinner's prayer is not enough. Church attendance will not suffice. Biblical knowledge will not save you.

In Scripture Christ refers to himself as the Bridegroom and to us as His bride. Without commitment, there is no marriage. Without relationship, there is no eternal life. In the last few words of 1 John 4:16, John tells us that the longer we live in God, the more our love grows perfect. Since Scripture uses the context of Christ as the bridegroom and us as His bride, let's look at marriage as an example. I have witnessed many times the progression and maturity between couples throughout their married life. The longer the marriage, the more they seem to relate as one rather than two separate individuals. They know each other inside out. They learn things about each other that they had no idea about until after they had been married for some time. One person can start a sentence, and their mate could finish it for them. They know how each other will react to different circumstances in life. They know what will make them happy, what makes them sad. They know ahead of time how they will handle adversity in the relationship. They literally come to a place where they become an extension of the other person. I have found in some cases with couples that have been married for years that they even begin to look alike. This kind of marriage can only take place when both persons are fully committed to each other.

So it is when we truly seek an unbroken relationship with God. The longer we walk *in* God the more we think and respond as God would respond. Our love and commitment to Him grows over time.

Peter addresses the importance of growing in God in 2 Peter 3:17 and 18. *"You already know these things dear friends. So be on guard; then you will not be carried away by the errors of these wicked people and lose your own secure footing. Rather, you must grow in the grace and knowledge of our Lord and Savior Jesus Christ."* First, let me emphasize once more that we are to grow *in* the knowledge of our Lord and not knowledge about Him. Second, if we are not growing, then our relationship stops growing and is stagnant in the same manner that a body of water becomes stagnant if it does not have a flow of fresh water feeding into it. Third, Peter makes it very clear in this passage that if we are not growing in our relationship with God, that we risk being carried away by wicked people and lose our own secure footing.

In my last book, *Seeking God's Truth in a Troubled World*,[1] I talked about a commitment I made to pray every morning that I would see with the eyes of Christ, that I would listen with the ears of Christ, and that I would speak with the lips of Christ. That was in response to Paul's directive in Philippians 2:5, *"You must have the same attitude that Christ Jesus had."* That is about as short and plain in the meaning as it can get. You cannot have an unbroken relationship without living *in* God and growing in your love and loyalty to Him. He has sent the Holy Spirit to us for just this reason.

---

[1] Richard Williams, *Seeking God's Truth in a Troubled World* (Cleveland, TN: Parson's Porch Books, 2023).

Chapter Nine

Growing in Grace

God saved you by His grace when you believed. And you can't take credit for this; it is a gift from God. Salvation is not a reward for the good things we have done, so none of us can boast about it. Ephesians 2:8 and 9

I am going to assume here that those who were interested enough to read this book are very familiar with this passage of Scripture in Ephesians 2:8 and 9. There is absolutely nothing that we do that earns us the right of salvation. If you are counting on your goodness to qualify you for God's grace, please read this passage again. If you are depending on your church attendance, please read the passage one more time. Even if you have been baptized into the faith and you are counting on that for your salvation, please read it again. Only the gift of God's grace to those who have become broken over their sin that has separated from God receive the gift of salvation. Once again, please do not hear me saying that those things are not important, for they are. They come about because of God's saving grace. They have no saving merit themselves.

Understanding God's grace and how it works in the life of the believer is greatly misunderstood by most Christians. I have heard many sermons over the years about *saving grace* where

85

God forgives our sins and gives us salvation. But grace is much more complex. When we do not understand its role in our life, we cannot walk in the power and the freedom that God's grace was intended for us. It is God's grace that empowers us to live victorious lives as well as extend His grace to others. Whenever God calls us to do something, or we find ourselves in a difficult situation, He will always supply the perfect measure of grace needed to represent Him well.

Here's a real-life example of grace shared by a friend. "In a men's Bible study one evening we broke into small groups of five to seven men after the initial teaching. Each man was to share his reflections on the teaching and share how he felt it should apply to his life that week. I felt that the teaching that night was specifically for me, as it pertained to the very things written about in this book. When my turn came to share, I spoke from my heart what the Lord had been showing me. One man in our group looked directly at me and strongly disagreed with what I felt the Lord was saying to me. I immediately felt my emotions rising up within me and I was ready to defend my position. It quickly transitioned from what had been a spiritual conversation into a conflict and battle of the wills. I was locked and loaded. Throughout the years in my profession, I have had to play an adversarial role either in court or with other authorities. As a result of those experiences, I am conditioned for this very type of conflicting argument. Needless to say, my response to my brother that evening could not be characterized as redemptive.

"Driving home that night I began to feel the heavy weight of guilt settling within my spirit. Unfortunately, the source of my guilt wasn't primarily because I had misrepresented God in my actions and response. At the heart of my guilt was my pride. I felt guilty because I thought the men would think less of me because of how I conducted myself."

This leads to the first point of receiving God's grace. The Bible tells us in James 4:7 that *"God resists the proud but gives grace to the humble."* The true source of all our conflicts in life is rooted in pride. I have dedicated an entire chapter (Chapter Eleven) to the subject of pride so I will not elaborate more.

So, what is grace and how does it work in the life of the believer? Most people think that grace is God's mercy toward us when we were sinners and that by His grace we are saved. Although that is true, it is just scratching the surface of understanding grace. The Bible goes on to instruct us in 2 Peter 3:18, to *"grow in grace."* We are to grow and mature in understanding and experiencing God's grace. It is essential to grow in grace if we truly desire an unbroken relationship with God the Father. Had my friend understood this truth during his conversation at the Bible study, he would have responded in grace rather than pride and God's grace would have been sufficient.

Grace is given to us by God to enable us to respond to the working of the Holy Spirit in our lives. When He gives us direction, He also gives us the desire and the ability to obey His direction. Then, and only then our relationship with God can deepen and become unbreakable. His grace is freely given, available at the point of need, and always sufficient. The amazing thing is that we reap a tremendous benefit from responding with God's grace. We are able to forgive even the most egregious sins against us, we have deeper fellowship with God the Father, and we have insights and wisdom that often saves us from failure or danger.

Back to my friend's example of grace. "As I continued to attend the men's Bible study, I eventually found myself paired with the same man that had opposed me. Once again, after sharing my insights he made quite a production of disagreeing with me. As expected, something began to rise up in me. However, this time the Holy Spirit tapped me on the shoulder and reminded me of my pride. This time I bowed my heart in agreement with the Holy Spirit and instantly received God's grace for that situation. It was something that I had never experienced in that way before. The working of God's grace in that moment instantly took away the inner conflict. I don't know how to explain it any other way. The inner conflict was replaced by peace and joy. That is the working of God's grace. It was available to me and when I received it, I immediately experienced it working. The good news is that grace is available to all. Whatever your conflicts in life may be, God's grace can replace the anxiety with inner peace that passes human understanding."

What would the outcome have been if my friend had not responded with God's grace to the brother who disagreed with him? He would have forfeited that inner peace that God had made available. The Bible addresses that as well. It is possible to resist and or miss God's grace. *"See to it that no one fails to obtain the grace of God; that no 'root of bitterness' springs up and cause trouble, and by it many become defiled."* (Hebrews 12:15). If we continually resist His grace in our lives, we can actually forfeit it. He adds, "As my relationship with God deepens, I have become much more aware of God's grace that is available to me." When Paul asked the Lord for help with what he defined as the *"thorn in his side"*, God's response was *"my grace is sufficient."* There is nothing in life that you will ever face where God's grace is not sufficient to give you victory over it. God makes possible what we may think is impossible. At the very moment that the Holy Spirit gives direction, He also supplies the grace (both the desire and the power) to follow His direction and please God. But if we hesitate or question it for any length of time (referred to in Scripture as *"resisting God's grace"*), then we miss His grace for that situation. The upside of receiving His grace and the ability to obey Him grows as our relationship with God deepens.

One often used definition of grace is *God's riches at Christ's expense*. I like this definition. If you examine it closely, it is clear that God's riches have no limit and all those riches have been made available to you and me because of Christ' sacrifice on the Cross. They have been made available to us even though there is nothing in us that makes us worthy of them. Stop and think for just a few moments about what all God has made available to us through His Son's death on the cross.

The most valuable thing that God makes available to us is what we refer to as The Pearl of Great Price. If you ask the average church-goer what the most valuable thing they possess as a Christian is, most will answer "the forgiveness of sin and eternity in heaven." Those are certainly very valuable things we inherit as believers but far from the most valuable thing available to us. That most valuable thing is God himself. We have available to us a close and direct relationship with the Creator of the universe.

Yet there are very few of us who tap into what God has made available. In short, that is the ability to live in complete victory in this life no matter what life may throw at us. Prior to understanding that the Pearl of Great Price and the Hidden Treasure is the relationship with God, I never really sensed anything separating myself from Him in the way I sense it now. The closer and deeper our relationship with God grows, the greater our desire grows to maintain that unbroken relationship with Him. But it is something that each one of us had to experience for ourselves. As we learn how to receive grace and experience the benefits, we begin to grow in grace as God commanded us to.

As our relationship with God grows, our motivation becomes to please Him. It is a real heart transplant. It happens because of the work of grace in our lives. As it happens, we pass from death to life, and we are set free! All things really do become new, and we begin to experience a peace that passes understanding and a joy unspeakable. Our former efforts to overcome sin are no longer needed in the same way because all our attention and efforts are focused on the relationship with

God. All this happens because of God's grace at work in our lives

Grace is that dynamic, divine power that not only allows us to have a relationship with God but will lead us to a place of an unbroken relationship with God; that position where we live in His presence twenty four hours a day where His thoughts become our thoughts, and His ways become our ways. We come to that place where we truly have the mind of Christ. It is God's grace that gives us both the desire and the power to do God's will. We often fail to access the power of God's grace because we have been taught that as long as we are in these mortal bodies we can never fully operate as a spiritual person. If we accept that as truth in our lives, we will never be able to experience that unbroken relationship that God intends for us to share with Him.

As we respond to God's grace we grow in our relationship with Him. As the relationship grows, we begin to experience the greatest motivation of our lives. That motivation is fully knowing God Himself and walking with Him in that unbroken relationship. The desires of our life begins to change. Instead of looking to God for the blessings we can receive from Him, we seek ways to be a blessing to Him. Our motives are no longer inwardly focused on what I want or need to an outward focus on what God wants of me. Even our attitude toward others changes to caring more about what others need rather than my own needs. This is exactly what Paul was speaking of when he told the Philippians, *"Don't be selfish; don't try to impress others. Be humble, thinking of others more highly than yourselves."*

(Philippians2:3-5). There is a command in that passage of Scripture as well; be humble. I will not say a lot here about humility as we cover it in the chapter on pride. But it must be noted here that in order to walk in the fullness of God's grace, it requires a humble heart and a humble spirit. To reach that unbroken relationship it requires living a Christlike life. I have made the following statement many times in my life, "all that matters to me is that when I lay my head on my pillow at night is to know that God is pleased with the way I lived that day."

How does God's grace work in our lives? Here are five aspects of His grace and how it works moment by moment within us:

1. We are given a measure of grace at the start of our relationship with Christ. *"Unto every one of us is given grace according to the measure of the gift of God."* (Ephesians 4:7). That is the grace given to us through Christ's death on the cross which brings the forgiveness of our sins allowing us to become a part of the family of God.

2. We are then told to grow in that grace. *"But grow in grace, and in the knowledge of our Lord and Savior Jesus Christ."* (2Peter 3:18). Nothing in all of life grows without proper nourishment. Without proper care and nutrients everything eventually dies. It is no different with our spiritual lives. Spiritual nutrients come by spending time building that personal relationship with God. A proper amount of time spent personally with Him, in His Word, in prayer, thinking of what He desires of me, and listening and discern what His will is for my life. Without these

things we will never reach the place of an unbroken relationship. We will settle for religious routine and convince ourselves either that is enough, or that we can never hope for more in this life.

3. His grace is always available. *"And God is able to make all grace abound toward you: that you always have sufficiency in all things and abound to every good work."* (2 Corinthians 9:8). God anxiously awaits to freely give His grace to anyone who desires to walk in it, and to live it out.

4. His grace is always sufficient. *"My grace is sufficient for you; my strength is made perfect in your weakness."* (2 Corinthians 12:9). Our tendency as Christians is to hide our weaknesses or pretend that they do not exist. Others just accept the fact that they are human, and the weaknesses are a part of living the Christian life here on earth. Yet Paul is sending a message to the church at Corinth, the most dysfunctional church of His day, that if they will bring those weaknesses to the Lord that they can be made perfect. We either decide to wear a mask and pretend we are better than we really are, or we bring the weaknesses to God and allow Him to exchange them for perfection.

5. We can resist grace. *"You stubborn people! You are heathen at heart and deaf to the truth. Must you forever resist the Holy Spirit? That is what your ancestors did, and so do you!"* (Acts 7:51). The Holy Spirit calls us by God's grace. Thus, to resist the Holy Spirit is to resist God's grace.

The essence of God's grace is found in the following verse: 2 Corinthians 5:21. *"For God made Christ, who never sinned, to be the offering for our sin, so that we could be made right with God through Christ."* God treated Christ like He was Richard Williams, and He treated me as if I were Jesus Christ. Now when He sees me, He sees the righteousness of His Son in me! Often people will say that they are not worthy, or that they are just poor sinners saved by grace. When you make that statement, you are saying in affect that God's grace and the power of the blood of Christ is not strong enough to cleanse you from the sin in your life. People who believe that do not know who they truly are in the Lord because of His grace.

Grace is the working of the Holy Spirit in our lives where He gives us both direction and the desire to please God in order to maintain an unbroken relationship. The ultimate reward in our relationship with God is that we receive His grace and walk in obedience and holiness. We get closer to Him. He reveals Himself more and more each day. The very motivation of our hearts changes to pleasing Him above all else.

Chapter Ten

Death of the Sinful Nature

Those who are dominated by the sinful nature do sinful things, but those who are controlled by the Holy Spirit think about things that pleases the Spirit. So, letting your sinful nature control your mind leads to death. But letting the Spirit control your mind leads to life and peace. Romans 8:5 -14

In Romans chapter seven, Paul had been addressing the realization that he could not overcome his sinful nature on his own. He was one of the most sincere and dedicated followers of Christ who has ever lived. Yet no matter how hard he tried he was caught in the vicious cycle of striving, struggling, repenting, and repeating. If he was ever going to overcome this endless merry-go-round he was going to need help. He could not do it by his own effort no matter how hard he tried, or how much he wanted to. This struggle with the sinful nature was just too much for even a man of strong committed faith like Paul. You simply cannot overcome it by your own human effort no matter how much you desire to do so. Paul was not saying that the sinful nature could not be overcome. Rather he is making the case for a total surrender to God, and to allowing the Holy Spirit, instead of our sinful nature to control our minds.

I struggled with Paul's message here in Romans 7 and 8 for many years. I have heard the explanations of these passages from two viewpoints. The first one says that because we are human, we can never overcome the sinful nature. The second viewpoint states, if you are filled with the Holy Spirit, you will never sin again. The fact is that the truth of Paul's testimony here lies in the middle of these two points of view.

Paul is telling us in this Romans 8 passage that God has made everything we need to overcome our old sinful nature, available to us through Christ's sacrifice on the cross. This is also supported by 2 Peter 1:3, *"By His divine power, God has given us everything we need for living a godly life. We have received all of this by coming to know Him, the one who called us to himself by means of His marvelous glory and excellence. And because of His glory and excellence, he has given us great and precious promises. These are the promises that enable you to share his divine nature and escape the world's corruption caused by human desires [our sinful nature]."* Those riches have been made available to us even though there is nothing in us that makes us worthy of them. Stop and think for just few moments of all God has made available to us through His Son's death on the cross.

We began Chapter One of this book with this statement and a haunting question, "I had hungered and thirsted for most of my life, but something was missing. The Bible talks about spiritual victory, why could I not obtain and sustain it?" I am confident that many Christians are asking themselves that question. There are thousands sitting in church week after week wondering, is this all there is? We hear great sermons about Christ and His ability to take away the sins of the world. We are told that with the power of the Holy Spirit there is nothing that we as believers cannot accomplish. Jesus even told us that if we had the faith of a mustard seed that we could move mountains. Yet we cannot overcome our own sinful habits, or sinful thoughts and deeds. In my early Christian ministry, I was a pastor for several years. I preached sermons that I knew were Biblically sound about victorious living in Christ. et secretly, I struggled to understand why I could not consistently live in the victory I preached about. To convince myself that I was the man God wanted me to be, I bought into the belief that as long as I was in this human body, I could never overcome my sinful nature. Years ago, there was a comedian named Flip Wilson who coined the phrase *the devil made me do it*. That was me in a nutshell. Since I was only human, I could not overcome sin in my life and that must be okay with God. All I could do was to try harder which worked, that is until I sinned again. All I could hope for was to continue the struggle and try again. One of Satan's greatest tools he uses against us is deception. I had been deceived to believe that I could never have complete victory over my sinful nature, at least not in this life. I was exactly where Paul was at in Romans 7. No matter how hard I might try, my sin was always right around the corner. I would tell myself repeatedly that after all, I am just human and as long as I am here on this earth I cannot overcome that sinful nature within me. Yet deep in my Spirit I could not accept that this was the best God could do for me or expect that He desired from me. I began to look back over my life and I have discovered that every time I have ever committed sin in my life, I had a choice. I have now walked with the Lord for over fifty years. I have had ample opportunity to ask myself that question. As I sit here this very moment taking inventory of the times that I have allowed my sinful nature to control my actions, I cannot think of a single solitary time that I did not have a choice in the matter. There is never a time in the life of a believer that you do not have a choice to either be controlled by your sinful nature or to allow God's Holy Spirit to control you. Understanding this is essential to having an unbroken relationship with God the Father.

Paul had come to the realization that if he was going to have the type of relationship with God that he hungered for, he would have to allow himself to be controlled by the Spirit rather than himself. The outcome of who has the control was so serious that he goes on to warn us of the implications of not giving control of our minds to the Holy Spirit.

Before you dismiss what I am about to say, I urge you to read Paul's words in Romans 8:12 and 13, *"Therefore dear brothers and sisters, you have no obligation to do what your sinful nature urges you to do*. ***For if you live by its dictates you will die!*** (emphasis mine). *But if by the power of the Spirit you put to death the deeds of your sinful nature, you will live."*

Chapter One introduced the subject of hunger and thirst. I stated that just as our physical bodies had a built-in ability to hunger and thirst to sustain our bodies, we have the same response regarding our spiritual relationship to God. If we choose not to feed the physical body, it will die. So, it is with your spiritual life as well. I would prefer not to write about this point, realizing that many will close the book and not finish it. However, understanding how to have an unbroken relationship with God, I cannot avoid it. If you hunger and thirst for more of God, I beg you to keep reading. To understand what Paul was warning us about we must remember who Paul was writing this letter to. Romans chapter 1, verse 7 gives us the answer. *"To all who are in Rome,* **beloved of God, called to be saints."** (emphasis mine). He is warning the beloved of God, the saints of God, that if they fail to feed their spiritual life, they will face death.

I repeat my statement from the first chapter. If you desire more in your relationship with God, if you want a continuous relationship with the Creator, this is where it must begin. It must begin with hungering and thirsting for the things of God. And it must lead to dying to our sinful deeds if we are to gain that unbroken relationship. Let me give you a modern-day parable. A couple fall in love and decide to get married. They express that they want to spend the rest of their lives together. Shortly after they have said their wedding vows and have lived together for a short time a problem arises. The husband makes the statement that he did not realize that he would have to give up seeing other women when he married his wife. Although his wife was his best friend and he wanted to remain married to her, he just didn't understand having to give up his former life. He was willing to provide for his wife by making a living, providing for food and shelter, going places and doing things with her. That is what the marriage meant to him. However, to expect that he would quit seeing his old girlfriends, or not hang out with *the boys* every night was just ridiculous. That would be asking him to change who he had always been. He simply would not give that up. My question to you would be, "Would you expect the spouse to stay in a relationship with a man who continues adulteress relationships with other women?" Is that what a true unbroken relationship looks like? Yet that is exactly how so many approach their relationship with God. I want to go to heaven, I want to be a Christian, but don't expect me to change. I want to enjoy those things here on earth while I am here. I will give it up when I get to heaven.

When we surrender to God, we experience a spiritual birth. When a baby is born, it must be nourished and cared for to become healthy and strong. To ignore it, or fail to care for it, the best you could hope for would be a dysfunctional and or sickly child. The worst case would be that the child dies for lack of care. This is exactly what Paul was referring to when he stated in Romans 8:6, *"Those who are dominated by the sinful nature think about sinful things, but those who are controlled by the Holy Spirit think about things that please the Spirit. So, letting your sinful nature control your mind* **leads to death.** *"* (emphasis mine). *But letting the Spirit control your mind leads to life and peace."* This is the essence of an unbroken relationship with God.

Chapter Eleven

Pride

First pride then the crash, the bigger the ego, the harder the fall. Proverbs 16:18 (The Message)

Keep in mind that the purpose of this book is to understand that Christ's death on the cross was to restore us to a full and right relationship with God the Father. The forgiveness of our sins was the initial act in that process. The problem arises when we believe that this is the completion of the Christian experience when it is bridge to the real reason Christ came - to restore that broken relationship with God the Father, one that never has to be broken again. Christ did not come just to die for the sin in our lives, but the root cause of that sin as well. That brings us to a discussion about pride.

As I have taken this journey in search of what I call an unbroken relationship with God, I have concluded that pride is synonymous with sin. The source of most, if not all conflicts between us and God, is rooted in pride. It began with man wanting to be as important as God. For many of us, we want to be Christians on our own terms and not on God's. If we are totally honest, the reason it upsets us to hear that we can live above sin, is that we don't want to give it up and not that we can't.

When I began preparation to write this chapter I thought back over those times in my life where I was failing God miserably.

I want to be fully transparent here, realizing that I run the risk of losing the faith and confidence that many have put in me throughout the years. Others will no doubt be reading this, and at this point will put the book down and walk away. However, if my true purpose is to demonstrate that God is more powerful in your life than anything else, this is part of that journey for me.

First, let me quote a passage from Paul. *"Don't be selfish, don't try to impress others. Be humble, thinking of others as better than yourselves."* (Philippians 2:3). Paul has pretty much framed the definition of pride with this one verse.

I want to focus on the last part of that verse for just a few moments. This is an area of pride that is literally destroying the very foundation of who we are supposed to be as God's witness here on earth. It has become so prevalent within the body of Christ that to even mention we are Christians brings out anger from those who we are speaking to. On top of that, we even take pride in how we have just *stood up* for God!

I am writing about those who pass judgement on others for the sin we see in their lives. They stand up to bring condemnation upon those whom they see as less spiritual than themselves. We know the Scriptures command us not to pass judgement upon others so we convince ourselves that we are just calling out their sin in order that the Holy Spirit can bring conviction upon them. These so-called crusaders of God come to believe that the Holy Spirit cannot do the job alone, and therefore we must call it out on His behalf. Now, if that is not pride, I do not know what is. They raise themselves up to be God's example of what true spirituality is, and in doing so they think of themselves as more highly than they should. If you stop and think about that one, it is not so much different from Satan wanting to be recognized as God. Misplaced Christian pride is one of the greatest reasons we are losing our credibility with those who are looking for the real answers of life.

Let me give some examples of what I am referring to with the hopes that you actually *feel* what it is that happens in these circumstances.

I want to be fully transparent here by telling you that this first example is about me. I have already touched on this in other writings, but I want to try and expose my heart in how I was impacted as a young sixteen-year-old boy. I knew as teenager that God had called me to not just be a Christian in name only, but that I would represent Him in everything I did in life. One of the first things I did was to find a church and a pastor that I could trust and allow to pour into my spiritual development. Although I had no doubts about what God was wanting to do within me, I was still a baby in Christ and knew little or nothing about how to walk it out. I came to love and trust this pastor and other mentors literally with my soul. These were people that I didn't just see on Sunday morning, they were my lifeline in learning how to walk with God. I soaked it up like a sponge.

Then came the night that our neighbor asked my father if he could loan me his car to go to the prom. I was excited and looked forward to one of the highlights of a teenager in high school. It would be a night that I would remember for the rest of my life, but it was not the kind of memory I had in mind. Sitting at the intersection of Race Street and Hwy 67 it happened. A drunk driver lost control of his car hitting me at a high rate of speed on the left front of my neighbor's car. He had left a bottle of whiskey under the driver's seat which burst upon impact. Imagine the smell of blood, anti-freeze, and whiskey all mixed together. My girlfriend and I spent several days hospitalized with severe injuries. My room was positioned where I could see visitors coming and going through the front entrance. I still remember the excitement I felt the first time I saw my pastor enter the hospital. It would only be a few minutes, and he would be in to pray with me and give me encouragement. I needed it since I was laying there with guilt that both me and my girlfriend almost died in the accident. It was definitely a time of reflection. Those few minutes turned into a half hour, then more than an hour. Soon I saw him exit the hospital without seeing me at all. I watched as this scenario played out day after day. My father was with me one day as this happened and I asked him why the pastor was not visiting me. Here was his response. I remember it as clearly as it was the day he said it fifty-seven years ago. "Son, they think you were drunk and almost killed a deacon's daughter." Never mind that I was given a blood test by the State Trooper investigating the accident indicating no alcohol present. Even if I had been drinking is not the point. When I was at one of the lowest points of my early life and needed God's people more than ever, I was not worthy of their Christian love anymore. They thought of themselves more highly than a sixteen-year-old boy needing God's love. That led to twelve years of wandering in darkness, filled with anger and rage. If this was the best God had to offer, not only did I not want it anymore, but I would also do everything in my power to expose the hypocrisy. Thankfully, after years of wandering in my own wilderness, God brought a genuine Christian into my life that lovingly and patiently showed me the way back. There is not a day in my life that I do not call out the name of Mike Boling and thank God for bringing him into my life. I have done that for fifty-five years.

The point I am trying to make is that when we are on the outside looking in at others, we never have the full story. Our role is to love these people into the Kingdom of God, not judge them out of it. It is the epitome of pride to place myself in the judgement seat that is reserved for God alone.

Several years ago, I received a phone call from my previous pastor in my home church in Arkansas. Several events had happened between the church and my pastor to the point that the church was on the brink of being divided in half, or risking closing altogether. Since I had many friends who were on opposite sides of the conflict, he was asking me to try and bring peace between the fractured sides. In hindsight, what he was really wanting was for me to take his side and get the opposing members to see his side or leave. I agreed to come under one condition. I would listen to all sides and in the end after much prayer and seeking God's wisdom make my recommendation as I felt God leading.

Upon my arrival I found a very angry and divide congregation. Most people had made up their minds. They had lost all faith and confidence that the pastor could lead effectively any longer. This was hard for me to believe as this man of God had founded more churches in his lifetime than some entire denominations do in a hundred years! I also discovered that after a lengthy and painful battle with cancer his wife of over fifty years had passed away. He had been at a very low point in his walk with the Lord and when he needed the body of Christ the most, they were ready to stone him. When there was no one to walk beside him through his pain and depression he made some unwise decisions. One was to remarry a very attractive *church-going* woman with grown children. Trouble began to arise very quickly. He did not seek counsel from his deacons and elders as he had chosen to marry a decent woman. However, she was not ready or willing to assume the role of a pastor's wife. Her children gave no respect to him as the spiritual leader of the home, nor would the wife come to the defense of her new husband.

Most of the congregation had loved the pastor's first wife and were loyal to her even after her death. They were angry with the pastor and felt he was being unfaithful to his deceased wife. It became very clear to me that the only solution to saving the church was for the pastor to resign and do what he was gifted to do - raise up another congregation and lead even more people to the Lord. Simply put, the congregation had come to the place that they could no longer think of their pastor more highly than they thought of themselves. They were going to be right and regardless of the damage that would follow.

I dreaded having my next conversation with my pastor, knowing it would be painful for him to hear what I had to say. I had known this man to be a lover of people and one who would do anything for the good of the people he was called to serve. That's what made what I would hear so difficult for me to believe. "Richard, I will stand at the doors of the church until I am the last man standing. They can chain the doors and put a padlock on them, and I will not leave!" This man of God whom I loved dearly had also lost sight of thinking of others more highly than himself.

Pride had consumed both sides to the point that the entire city was now witnessing the destruction of a spiritual pillar of the community. My pastor and friend never led another congregation. Many of the congregants left the church and never connected with another body of believers. Not long ago, my pastor died, a lonely and broken man. Pride had won.

Here's another example: I recently had the opportunity to attend a men's Saturday morning prayer group. They came together every Saturday to pray for the church services and leadership for the upcoming Sunday. I found it amazing that the men of the church would make this sacrifice to gather at six every Saturday morning to pray for their leadership and the people who would enter the doors of the church. I accompanied one of the Sunday School teachers as he went into his empty classroom and prayed over every empty chair knowing that within a few hours someone would be sitting in that very chair.

But what I remember most about that Saturday morning is when one of the men shared the history of that group. It apparently had been formed by a very Christ-centered individual who was committed to lifting up the leadership as well as all who would enter the church each week. Under his leadership dozens of men would turn out each Saturday to join him in praying that God would anoint the leaders, that people would find Christ, and that God himself would be glorified. One man in the group had different aspirations. He eventually became the new leader of the group and made a statement that went something like this: "It is time that the old guard step aside so that the group could move forward with new and fresh ideas." The number of men attending quickly dropped from several dozen each week to just a handful of faithful men who came for the fellowship. The focus of those Saturdays changed from an outward focus to one of an inward focus. It changed to a time with long devotional and a brief prayer time. The power and presence of the Holy Spirit was hard to find. One prideful statement is all it took to suck the life out of the group. I love the way Eugene Peterson says it in the Message. *'First pride, then the crash – the bigger the ego, the harder the fall.'* (Proverbs 16:18).

The ways in which pride tries to come between us and God are countless. Pride will cripple our relationship with God, as well as with those around us. Much like a leech seeks to suck the blood life right out of our bodies, pride will suck every ounce of spiritual life that we have with God and those around us. There is not one single solitary person who has ever lived on this earth that has not had to deal with what the Bible calls, *"the pride of life."* (I John 2:16).

Many Christians never reach the full blessings God has for them because the sin of pride holds them back. We certainly cannot have that unbroken relationship with God the Father until we deal with the pride in our lives.

We have areas of pride in our lives that we are not even aware of. Sometimes it's even that we think that we are being spiritually loyal to God and our personal convictions. A few years ago, a young person was struggling with their sexual identity. They were confused, afraid, and no doubt many times contemplated suicide. They desperately needed the love and counsel from the church they were attending. Instead, the church *shunned* this young and impressionable soul. The church did not want this confused and depressed person contaminating the other youth in the church. Instead of thinking of this individual more highly than themselves, or reaching out with patience and love, they judged and condemned him. Eventually this young person was able to work through their struggles and find their true identity as God had intended, despite so-called holy people of the church. The sad ending to the story is that although this person had overcome their confusion about identity, they had no use for God or His people. By thinking of themselves more highly than others, they shut the kingdom of heaven off for this precious soul. They will account for their sin.

When people are struggling with various sins in their lives, whether it is sexual identity, addiction, illicit affairs, or a host of other sinful challenges, we have a choice. We can patiently love them into the Kingdom of God, or we can judge them out of it. One shows humility, the other is rooted in pride.

"God resists the proud but gives grace to the humble." (James 4:6). The word resist in the Greek translates "go to battle against." God feels so strongly about pride in our lives as Christian that He will go to war against us to defeat it in our lives. God realizes that the sin of pride can destroy every aspect of life. Pride can destroy the family home. It will forever stand between a husband and wife, or a parent and a child. The sin of pride keeps a husband or wife from apologizing when they are wrong. The failure to apologize when wrong breeds contention and disunity between the couple. Pride will prevent a believer from having that uninterrupted, ongoing relationship that God desires, to the point that He will go to war to defeat it.

Pride is hell-bent on winning the argument even at great cost. Instead of winning the argument, the Spirit-filled believer will focus on resolving the conflict. Once conflict is resolved peace will flood your heart and mind like a gentle wind.

In summary, 1 John2: 15 and 16, *"For all that is in the world, the lust of the flesh, the lust of the eyes, and the pride of life, is not of the Father but is of the world. And the world is passing away, and the lust of it; but he who does the will of God abides forever."*

Chapter Twelve

Living for Christ

Either way, Christ love controls us. Since we believe that Christ died for all, we also believe that we have died to our old life. He died for everyone so that those who receive His new life will no longer live for themselves. Instead, they will live for Christ, who died and was raised for them. 2 Corinthians 5: 14 and 15

In an unbroken relationship with God the Father, control of my life is turned over to Christ. If you look up the definition of the word control here is what you will find. "It is the power to direct one's behavior or the course of events." (Cambridge dictionary). Paul is stating that we no longer take charge of the direction of our lives but instead allow God to take total control. He charts the course my life takes, and I follow that course one hundred percent without doubt or question. In Genesis 12 we find a great example of this. God appeared to Abraham and told him to leave his native country, and all his relatives. Abraham did not try and justify why he should not leave his family; he just went because he had given God control of his life. Imagine God telling you to leave the comfort of your home, leave family and friends behind, and set out to somewhere foreign to you. Do you trust Him enough to influence your life and your future that you would do it? For me it was leaving the comfort of my southern lifestyle to the inner city of Chester and Philadelphia, PA. Had I not allowed

God to control my future this book would not be written by me, and if I had it would have no credibility. Had Abraham not allowed control of his life to God the nation of Israel would not exist today.

The greatest example of giving control of life over to God is Christ himself. Agonizing over His torture, his impending separation from the Father, followed by being nailed to a cross, He was still able to say, *"not my will but Your will be done."* (Luke 22:42 KJV). Without that surrender of control there would be no redemption from sin for you and me.

Have you given that control over to God? Control that allows Him to direct your paths. We see this played out over and over with the spiritual giants of Scripture. It was allowing God to direct his path that Joseph could accept all the things that happened to him and to say, *"You intended to harm me, but God intended it all for good."* (Genesis 50:20). Instead of getting revenge against his brothers, he was able to forgive them and understand why God allowed those things to happen in his life.

Throughout Paul's writings he repeatedly talks about putting to death our old lifestyle. When we come to the place where we are fully walking in that unbroken relationship with God, we no longer even desire to live for ourselves. Each moment of everyday it is about living for Him. We are now defining the word *unbroken* when it comes to how we relate to God.

Total control cannot be given to God unless we are willing to die to ourselves as Paul says to the Corinthians. To gain that unbroken relationship with God we must be willing to live for Christ. We must come to a place as Abraham did that although he did not know all the facts, he got up and moved simply because God directed him to do so. We must be willing like Christ to say, *"not my will but your will be done."*

If you truly want to have a deep intimate relationship with God, one where His presence is so real that you are consciously aware of Him every minute of every day, it will require that you really die to yourself and allow Him to completely live in you and take control. Read the words of Jesus in Mark 12:30. *"The most important commandment is this: Listen O Israel, the Lord our God is the one and only Lord. And you must love the Lord your God with all your heart, all your soul, all your mind, and all your strength."* Jesus is telling us that nothing is more important in the Christian life than giving our all to Him. Those who have been through my seminars on discipleship have heard me say that those who get you to say a sinner's prayer and then walk away have often just sent people on a path straight to hell. I watch television preachers tell those watching that if they just *repeat after me* a simple prayer that they just were saved. If there is no understanding of what true repentance is, they have been given a false hope in regard to eternity. If there is no brokenness, no sense of shame on the part of the one praying the prayer, the motive of their prayer is misplaced. Most importantly, if there is no desire for a genuine relationship with God they pray in vain.

If you are counting on a sinner's prayer alone for salvation you are going to be among those whom God says, *"I never knew you."*

God wants you, not your religious practices that many proclaim as salvation. He wants you, all of you - heart, mind, body and soul. He wants a real relationship with you, and nothing less than your all will satisfy Him. That is what it means to die to self and come alive in Christ. That is when we can claim the promise He gave us, that He would never leave us or forsake us - the essence of an unbroken relationship.

Chapter Thirteen

Divine Power

His divine power has granted to us all things that pertain to life and godliness, through the knowledge of Him who called us to His own glory and excellence.
2 Peter 1:3

Your circumstances in life should never dictate where you are in your relationship with God. Yet for so many that is exactly what they allow to happen. That is at least in part, what this book has been about. To walk so closely with God that the circumstances of your life cannot cause you to doubt or even become angry at God. Our relationship is unbreakable. Your faith, your trust, the fact that God is with you, is what brings victory in you.

Paul discovered the true meaning of an unbroken relationship with God. Note carefully what he says in Romans 8:35-39. *"Can anything ever separate us from Christ love? Does it mean that he no longer loves us if we have trouble or calamity, or are persecuted or hungry, or are destitute, or are in danger, or threatened with death? ... No, despite all these things, overwhelming victory is ours through Christ, who loved us. And I am convinced that nothing can ever separate us from God's love. Neither death nor life, neither angels or demons, neither our fears for today, nor our worries about tomorrow - not even the powers of hell can separate us from God's love. No power in the sky above or the earth below - indeed, nothing in all creation will ever be able to separate us from the love of God that is revealed in Christ Jesus our Lord!"*

These were words that came from a man who had endured more than you and I will ever have to endure. Five times he was given thirty-nine lashes with a whip, three times beaten with a rod. He had been stoned, shipwrecked three times, and many of his own race rejected him. Many times, he almost starved to death for lack of food and water and shivered in the cold. Yet, despite all these things, Paul could say, *"overwhelming victory is mine through Christ who loves me!"*

That is the testimony of a man who defined the very heart of an unbroken relationship with God. There are those who interpret this that God will never leave us, and that is true. However, it is only half of the message it contains. Paul was speaking from his own walk with the Lord. Whenever adversity surrounded him, it was his unbroken relationship with God that sustained him. He was telling us that no circumstances of life would ever break the bond of that relationship.

Everything that goes into a life of pleasing God has been miraculously given to us by getting to know personally and intimately, the One who invited us to God.

As Christians we need to understand that we are, right now, fully equipped to have that unbroken relationship with God. Paul and Peter both, two men who suffered greatly for their faith in God, had learned how to walk in that unbroken relationship with God.

The unbroken relationship is quickened within us by the power of God's Word and the fullness of the Holy Spirit living within us. Everything changes; the way we think, the words we speak, and the actions we take. We begin to think with the mind of God and not our own. The words we speak are directed by God and not by our flesh. Finally, the actions we take are the actions of God. When others look upon us, they do not see a mere human, they see the result of God living and alive within us. Our actions are the testimony of the power of God at work within us.

We have completely died to our old self and the power of sin that so easily disrupted our relationship with God, no longer has control over us. As Paul said in 2 Corinthians 5:17 *"Old things have passed away, and all things have become new."*

We have successfully transitioned from that life of striving, stumbling, repenting, and repeating. We have entered that inner sanctuary behind the curtain of the Holy of Holies where Christ waits to consummate the unbroken relationship with us. I want to close this chapter and the book by giving special thanks to Dave Hunt who tirelessly read through multiple rewrites of this book in order to present to you as flawless a copy as possible. I had been struggling with an appropriate ending to tie together all my thoughts included in my writings. Without knowing I was struggling to bring the book to an end, he provided me with that perfect ending in a message he sent to me the morning after we had completed all the edits and submitted the manuscript to the publisher. I am including here what Dave shared just as he wrote it to me.

"Richard, I just read this this morning from I Thessalonians 5:23-24(NLT). '*Now may the God of peace make you holy in every way and may your whole spirit and soul and body be kept blameless until our Lord Jesus Christ comes again. God will make this happen for He who calls you is faithful.*' It really hit me hard this morning after spending much time in your book. Three things stood out:

> 1. God makes us holy; we do not make ourselves holy.
> 2. We are to be holy in every way.
> 3. He keeps our spirit, soul, and body blameless. He will make this happen, for He is faithful. Wow!"

Dave's comments sums up what the unbroken bond between you and God will look like. When we come to God spiritually hungry and thirsty, when we come to Him broken over the sinful life we have lived, ready to follow Him in obedience, God covers us with His holiness that only He can provide. May God bless you as you seek that *Unbroken Bond* with the King of all Kings.

Chapter Fourteen

Spiritual Warfare

For we do not wrestle against flesh and blood, but against the rulers, against the authorities, against the cosmic powers over this present darkness, against the spiritual forces of evil in the heavenly places.
Ephesians 6:12

Shortly after finishing the manuscript for this book, I began to think back over the challenges I faced in getting it written. I was sidelined with pneumonia, followed by being hospitalized with blood clots on my lungs. There were conflicts with extended family members that weighed heavily on my wife and me. A serious reduction in support has required us to adjust our lifestyle. Most heartbreaking was a disagreement with a brother that I love dearly.

Several years ago, our ministry with another organization I led suffered a very high-profile murder in our facility. It was in all the newspapers and television stations throughout the greater Philadelphia area. I was so despondent that I tried to resign as the leader, but the board would not accept my resignation. I was having a cup of coffee with one of the board members when he told me this: "Richard, do you realize that for Satan to do something of this magnitude the ministry had to be sitting dead center on the bullseye of God's will?"

Perhaps once again Satan wanted to stop me, this time from writing this book. The last thing the enemy wants is for Christians to discover a deep intimate relationship with God the Father; the kind of relationship that cannot be broken.

In writing to the church in Thessalonica, Paul expressed his desire to see them. He tried again and again to go but each time *"he was hindered by Satan."* (I Thessalonians 2:18). John tells us in his gospel that the thief comes to steal, kill, and destroy. Satan desires to destroy our love, our peace, and our joy. If he is successful, then he renders us powerless and ineffective.

There is a spiritual world out there that we cannot see. Although we cannot see it, does not mean that it does not exist. It is very real and the one who has temporary dominion over what Paul called this present darkness, seeks to destroy you. The wording almost sounds like something out of a Star Wars movie, but Paul tells us that he has cosmic powers. The ultimate goal of Satan is to destroy your spiritual life and claim your soul for a burning hell. Read Peter's words in 1 Peter 5:8. *"Be sober, be vigilant; because your adversary the devil walks about like a roaring lion, seeking whom he may devour."*

Having traveled throughout Africa in my ministry, I picked up an interest in watching documentaries about Africa wildlife. When I read Peter's analogy of Satan as a roaring lion, seeking to devour us, I imagined the African lion stealthy sneaking up on his unaware prey and viciously attacking at just the right moment. It is brutal, it is bloody, and it ends in death for the innocent prey. The lion then relaxes and begins to devour his freshly slaughtered victim. Fast forward and you will find the lion laying in the grass with an expression of satisfaction on his face for killing and devouring his game. This is how Peter describes what Satan desires to do to all God's people.

On the other side stands God and His angels ready to do battle for the sake of saving your soul. Note this real-life example in Daniel 10:12 and 13. *"The angel said, 'Fear not Daniel for from the first day that you set your heart to understand and humbled yourself before your God, your words have been heard, and I have come because of your words.'* <u>*The Prince of the Kingdom of Persia withstood me for twenty-one days*</u> (emphasis mine), *but Michael, one of the chief princes, came to help me, for I was left there with the kings of Persia, and came to make you understand what is to happen to your people in latter days, for the vison is for days yet to come."* Daniel had been crying out for answered prayer. The demons were trying to block the answer to his prayer making it feel on the surface that either God did not care, or worse that he was wanting Daniel to think God did not care enough to answer his prayer at all.

This chapter on spiritual warfare is being included to inform you, the reader, that whenever you decide that you desire to live in an unbroken relationship with God, Satan wants you to believe that it is impossible, or that God does not care for you enough to make it happen. He will use every tool in his arsenal to prevent it.

I have battled spiritual warfare just in getting this book to the finish line. There must be something here Satan does not want you to read, or more importantly, he does not want you to live by. The enemy will take extreme measures to come between you and God the Father. He wants to keep you a spiritual weakling and in the case of anyone who realizes that they have been living a religious life rather than having intimate relationship with God, his goal is to see that you never come to know Him. To be that person who stands before God with a host of spiritual things they have accomplished, God says *"I never knew you, depart from me"* (Matthew 7:23 KJV).